# ITALY
## THE HILLTOWNS

# ITALY
## THE HILLTOWNS

### JAMES BENTLEY

#### PHOTOGRAPHY BY
### JOE CORNISH

GEORGE
PHILIP

HALF-TITLE ILLUSTRATION
A sunlit courtyard in Città della Pieve.

TITLE-PAGE ILLUSTRATION
The eastern slopes of Enna.

# ACKNOWLEDGMENTS

I have many people to thank. They include Sig. A. Turiano, who is director of tourism at the Azienda Autonoma Soggiorno e Turismo, Taormina, Sicily; Dr Secondo Amalfitano, Assessore al Turismo, Comune di Ravello, Italy; the Ristorante Ravello, 45/48 Old Street, London EC1; Jennifer Paton, Marketing Director, the Magic of Italy, 227 Shepherd's Bush Road, London W6 7AS; Sig. Giancarlo Ronci, director of the Azienda di Promozione Turistica, Assisi; the Director, Azienda di Turismo, Piazza Duca Federico, Urbino; the staff of the Azienda Autonoma Soggiorno Turismo del Tuscolo; and Signorina Paola Greco of the Italian National Tourist Board in London.

*British Library Cataloguing in Publication Data*
Bentley, James 1937—
Italy: the hill towns.
1. Italy.—Visitor's guides
I. Title
914.504929

Text © James Bentley 1990
Photographs © Joe Cornish 1990
Maps © George Philip 1990

First published by George Philip,
59 Grosvenor Street, London W1X 9DA

Book design by Simon Bell

ISBN 0–540–01216–5

Typeset by Keyspools Ltd, Golborne, Lancashire

Printed in Italy

# CONTENTS

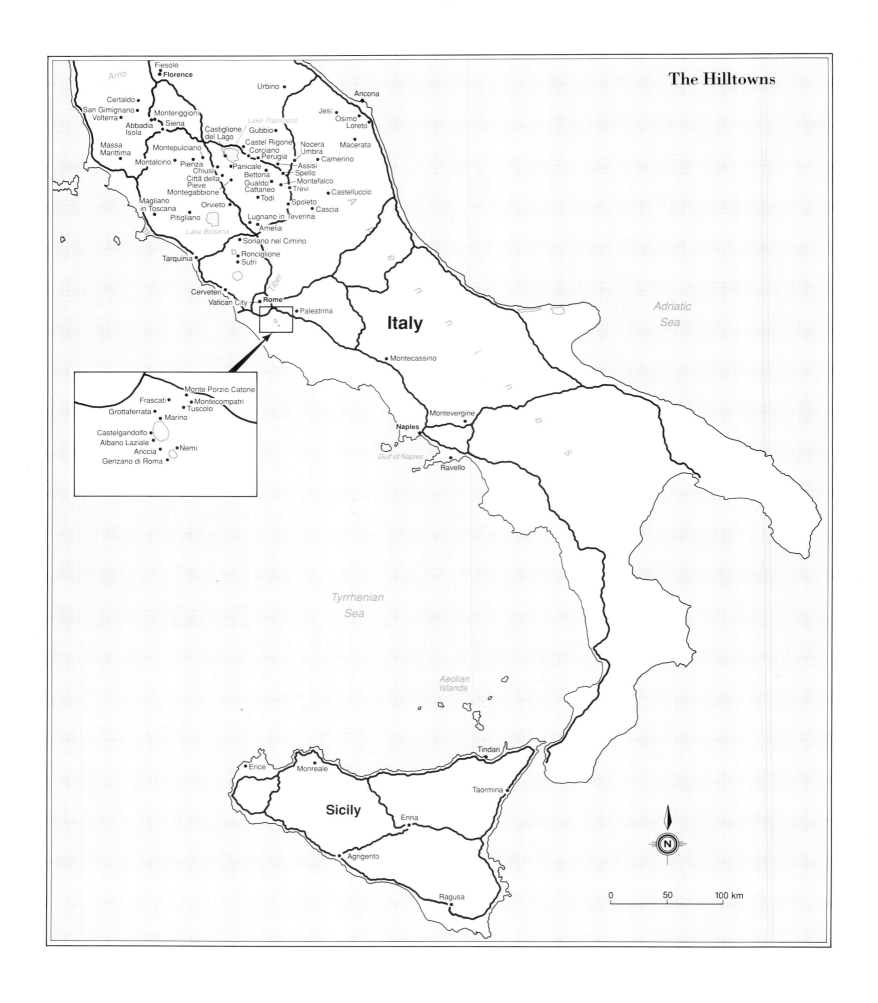

The Hilltowns

*Arno*
Fiesole
**Florence**
Urbino
Ancona
Certaldo
San Gimignano
Jesi
Volterra
Monteriggioni
Osimo
Loreto
Abbadia Isola
Siena
*Lake Trasimeno*
Gubbio
Castiglione del Lago
Massa Marittima
Montepulciano
Castel Rigone
Corciano
Nocera Umbra
Camerino
Macerata
Montalcino
Pienza
Perugia
Chiusi
Panicale
Assisi
Città della Pieve
Bettona
Spello
Montegabbione
Gualdo Cattaneo
Montefalco
Castelluccio
Magliano in Toscana
Todi
Trevi
Orvieto
Spoleto
Cascia
Pitigliano
Lugnano in Teverina
*Lake Bolsena*
Amelia
Tarquinia
Soriano nel Cimino
Ronciglione
Sutri
*Tiber*
Cerveteri
Vatican City
**Rome**
Palestrina

**Italy**

Montecassino

*Adriatic Sea*

Monte Porzio Catone
Frascati
Montecompatri
Tuscolo
Grottaferrata
Marino
Castelgandolfo
Albano Laziale
Ariccia
Nemi
Genzano di Roma

Montevergine
**Naples**
*Gulf of Naples*
Ravello

*Tyrrhenian Sea*

*Aeolian Islands*

Tindari
Erice
Monreale
Taormina
**Sicily**
Enna
Agrigento
Ragusa

N

0    50    100 km

# INTRODUCTION:
# CITIES SET ON HILLS

ITALY'S HILLTOWNS sum up all that is most enticing about the country: its history, art, architecture and natural beauty. The land is crammed with them in part simply because the contours of Italy are so convoluted, with the spiky backbone of the Apennines running down its centre and the Alps and Dolomites stretching along its northern frontier. Again, some four-fifths of Sicily consists of mountains or hills. The hilltowns rising on these undulating ranges are what bring people back again and again to Italy. A vision of red-tiled houses straggling up to a *castello* or *palazzo* high above, their whitewashed walls set off by finger-like cypresses, vineyards neatly laid out on the slopes below them, captures the essence of Italy.

Italian history has been marked by wars, invasions and internal struggles, all of them reflected in aspects of her hilltowns. Here too are preserved the religious face of romanesque architecture, and splendid gothic, renaissance or baroque palaces and churches, as well as a wealth of remains from ancient times. Southern Italy and Sicily were for centuries part of the Hellenic world, a region of Greek colonies whose Doric temples and superb amphitheatres still survive in today's hilltowns. From the seventh to the second century BC the Etruscans dominated central Italy, and they too built on hills, learning artistic skills from the Greeks but also fighting with their mentors. For a time Etruscan kings ruled Rome itself, and Roman remains surface in essentially Etruscan cities. Later the Normans were to take Sicily from the Arabs who had controlled it since the ninth century, stamping their own distinctive character on the face of the country. Norman rule was challenged in the twelfth and thirteenth centuries by the Hohenstaufen family, after the Hohenstaufen duke Frederick Barbarossa became Holy Roman Emperor in 1155. At the same time Frederick and his successors were in continual conflict with the papacy. Such struggles gave another powerful impetus to building fortified cities and towns on defensible hills, and many fortresses and palaces seen today are legacies of papal or imperial rule. This same conflict between emperor and pope ensured that no-one ruled supreme throughout Italy. Communes owing allegiance to no overlord vied with monarchies and duchies in amassing wealth and embellishing their hilltowns and cities, many of which developed into independent little capitals. By the end of the twelfth century, internal feuds and rivalries in many of these free communes led their citizens to appoint a supreme magistrate, the *podestà*. Like the great families, these officials proclaimed their status by building themselves fortified palaces and castles.

The Hohenstaufen Emperor Frederick II became King of Sicily in 1198. After his death in 1250, for a time Naples and Sicily were united under the French house of Anjou. The Sicilians ousted the Angevins in 1282, and a much greater impact on the hilltowns of the region was left by their successors, the Aragonese, the first of whom, Peter III of Aragon, claimed the throne because of his distant relationship with the Hohenstaufens. Into the architecture of Sicilian hilltowns was now inserted a new, Spanish element.

The Renaissance did not remove the need for military watchfulness. As a servant of the Duke of Urbino in the late fifteenth century, the humanist Baldassare Castiglione painted a picture of an ideal courtier in his book *Il Cortegiano* (1528) in which he insisted that 'the first and foremost true profession of a courtier must be to bear arms'. Yet a balance of power prevailed in Italy and Europe which brought an era of comparative peace. Fortresses could develop into palaces. Italy had led the European revival of trade which had begun in the eleventh century. The bankers of her city states were now dominant, and their wealth financed the transformation of many hilltowns according to the new principles of renaissance and later baroque architecture. The renaissance princes sometimes created cities on a hill simply to glorify themselves. For this purpose the humanist Pope Pius II rebuilt his birthplace Pienza, no doubt remembering the words of the Gospel (Matthew: XII.14) that a city set on a hill cannot be hid.

In spite of its great reverence for Greek and Roman antiquity, renaissance humanism by no means rejected the Christian religion. Baldassare Castiglione himself spent the last years of his life in Spain as Bishop of Avila and papal nuncio. Moreover, castles and fortresses were not enough to convince the men and women of Italy's war-scarred past that they were secure either in this world or the next. They needed some divine reassurance as well. In the words of the psalmist, recited in their churches and cathedrals, 'I will lay me down in peace and take my rest,' they believed, 'because it is thou Lord only that makest me to lie down in safety'. Long before Moses received the commandments of God on Mount Sinai, men and women had felt a numinous awe on mountain tops and many sites had long been considered holy ground. Hilltowns rendered sacred by the bones of saints were especially revered, and these spots, above all Assisi, became renowned places of pilgrimage, growing rich and building fabulous shrines on the wealth brought by the pilgrims.

Finally, the practical desire to avoid living in unhealthy marshlands was also a factor which drove people to settle atop the hills of Italy and to terrace the hillsides for vineyards and other crops.

The sites of all these hilltowns were chosen with great care, frequently protected from the east winds by surrounding mountains and often built on the warm western slopes of the hills. Their founders clearly relished superb panoramas, especially when these encompassed stretches of water. Where these waters included a harbour, a hilltown such as Ancona, strategically set on its promontory overlooking the sea, could become rich.

But whereas some Italian hilltowns surround fortresses and were created for

Romanesque urbanity: the façade of Santa Maria della Piazza, Ancona.

OVERLEAF LEFT
Poppies bloom in the fields below Nemi.

OVERLEAF RIGHT
An isolated hill village near Pievina, between Florence and Siena.

defensive reasons, while others cluster around churches (themselves sometimes fortified), all are welcoming. Those which sprang up on former holy sites where ancient temples stood fascinatingly reveal their ancient selves under the skills of archaeologists. So Palestrina, rising on Monte Ginestro outside Rome, is today most remarkable for the excavated Temple of Fortuna Primigenia, dating from the second century BC. The town's seventeenth-century *palazzo* rises from part of this venerable sanctuary; the rest (partly uncovered by the bombs of World War II) is open to view. Pushing on into the sanctuaries of the Christian era, the most fascinating characteristic of Tindari in Sicily is its centuries-long fame as a centre of devout pilgrimage.

Moulded by millennia of wars, invasions, religious passion, enormous wealth, monarchical ambition and the mundane concerns of the humble, these hilltowns offer a microcosm of western civilization scarcely found elsewhere. Many of them have become preserved at one moment in time, their architectural gems unspoilt over subsequent centuries. Some, such as the quintessential Etrusco-Roman hilltown of Tuscolo, survive without later buildings because they were abandoned. Others remain entrancing monuments from one era in the past, even though they have continued to be inhabited over the centuries. Thus Spello in Umbria is an exquisite romanesque town, Tuscan San Gimignano al Monte encapsulates perfectly the glories of the fourteenth century, while Ragusa on its double ridge in south-east Sicily is crammed with baroque palaces and churches.

Just as the reasons for setting on a hill were diverse, so the aspect of these towns varies remarkably. In Tuscany, for example, Massa Marittima once rose over the sea, until the coastline silted up. Today it divides itself into two parts, the *città vecchia*, whose cathedral is a Pisan romanesque masterpiece of the thirteenth century, and the *città nuova*, which boasts not only a ruined medieval fortress built by the Sienese but also a spiky gothic church dedicated to St Francis of Assisi. In Umbria by contrast, Lugnano in Teverina is a walled town so self-effacing that its romanesque church, Santa Maria Assunta, remains basically as it was in the twelfth and thirteenth centuries. The citizens have not yet replaced the wooden beams of its thirteenth-century portico with anything more substantial.

Some of the towns and cities included in this book are ancient, while others date only from the tenth or eleventh centuries. Many guidebooks misleadingly refer to these enchanting places as 'hilltop towns', misleadingly because several of them merely tumble down the sides of hills, whereas others clamber up them from the valleys but do not quite reach the top. Urbino (as the derivation of its name indicates) confounds them all by straddling not one but two ridges. I have focused on what I regard as the best of them, the ones that are relatively unspoilt (while also including, for example, Ancona, whose environs are certainly nasty but whose history and surviving treasures no-one should despise).

This book proceeds for the most part chronologically, though the towns and cities are also classified partly by their predominant architectural styles, partly by their historical associations and above all by the manner in which their history has affected their physical aspect.

# 1

# GREEKS, ROMANS AND
# ETRUSCANS

THE ANCIENT GREEKS themselves coined the phrase 'greater Greece' to describe the extent of their expansion into southern Italy in the eighth century BC. The decline of their maritime rivals, the Phoenicians, had given their ships freedom of the seas, and they set out to explore distant lands. Moreover, their own burgeoning population made such expansion a necessity. These sailors obviously loved to colonize those parts of Italy which overlooked the sea. Even before they left their homeland many such venturers had already appointed a single citizen to rule their planned colonies, but soon these tyrants were replaced by democratically elected representatives. The Greeks also brought their gods and goddesses, and their prophetesses or sybils. The most famous of the sybils lived in a cavern at Cumae near Naples. According to legend, Apollo had granted the Cumaean sibyl as many years on earth as she had grains of sand in her hand, but since she failed to ask to remain young, she shrivelled into a tiny, miserable creature, spending most of her time in a jar. Philosophers followed the deities, Pythagoras, for instance, leaving the Greek island of Samos around 521 BC to spend the rest of his life at Crotone in Calabria.

As for their towns, these were laid out in a regular pattern, adapted to the lie of the land. The *agora*, or market, and the temples usually occupied the high ground. The finest of such hilltowns, Agrigento in Sicily, has suffered the ravages of time, but only perhaps Volterra (see p. 19) can match the impact of this spot. Agrigento Basso, the industrialized new town at the bottom of the hill, is scarcely beautiful. No matter, for it is the ancient city which draws people here. As Lawrence Durrell insisted, from the point of view of natural beauty and elegance its site is 'easily a match for Athens on its hills'. Founded in 582 BC, it became rich and powerful in the next century, only to be crushed by Carthage in 406 BC. At its apogee some 100,000 persons are said to have lived here, building a succession of superb temples whose remains are the finest in Italy. The musician, poet, philosopher and doctor Empedocles was born here in the fifth century BC.

The Arabs who ruled the place in the ninth century (and incidentally brought pasta to Sicily) changed its name to Girgenti, and the city became Agrigento again only in 1927. To savour an initial flavour of its antiquity, find Santa Maria dei Greci, a twelfth-century Norman church built on the site of a Doric temple. Of the ten Greek temples constructed in the sixth or fifth century BC, nine survive, and this one, having been transformed into a Christian church, is the best preserved. The church, like Agrigento cathedral and some other parts of the medieval city, shows the wear and tear of the latest earthquake suffered here.

Agrigento's nineteenth-century quarter lies to the east, and beyond it stands the romanesque church of San Biagio. Not surprisingly, this church also displaced a Greek temple, and here appears the stupendous vista of the so-called archaeological quarter of the city. The scene is rendered all the more charming – even rustic – by pine trees, olives and almonds, by aloes and bougainvillias, the varied greens merging and contrasting with each other. The vista extends as far as the sea. Only in the heat of summer does this region lack flowers and vegetation. Below is the rocky sanctuary of Demeter and Persephone, which dates from the sixth century BC. Some contend that the building arose perhaps a century earlier, in which case the Greeks evidently took over the temple of a previous cult, adapting it to their goddess of vegetation, just as the Christians were to adapt for their own use the sacred buildings of the Greeks. Demeter still seems to influence the Christian festivals of Agrigento, for on the first Sunday of July, when the citizens celebrate the festival of San Caolgero, a donkey parades through the streets carrying sheaves of corn. Another donkey carries bread baked to represent the sick who have been healed by the intercessions of the Christian saint. Naturally, too, the people of Agrigento celebrate the flowering of the almond trees with another festival.

These ancient ruins were by no means abandoned after the Carthaginians destroyed the might of Agrigento. The main road that leads towards the valley of the temples passes on the left the remains of a Greco-Roman city, still retaining pavement mosaics and paintings, which was inhabited at least until the fifth century AD. On the right is the fourteenth-century church of San Nicola, where those who arrive in the morning (for the church is closed after noon) can view a celebrated sarcophagus (in the second chapel on the right) and relive Goethe's ecstatic response to its carvings. 'It portrays Hippolytus with his hunting companions and his horses,' he wrote. 'Phaedra's nurse has bidden them halt and is about to hand a little tablet to Hippolytus.' Then Goethe acutely added: 'The chief aim of the artist was to depict beautiful young men. In order not to distract from them he has carved the old nurse as a tiny woman, almost as a dwarf.' Goethe declared that he had never seen a bas-relief so wonderful or well-preserved. He took it to be Greek, though the sarcophagus is actually a second-century Roman masterpiece based on Greek examples.

Past a Greek amphitheatre you reach the Museo Archeològico, its legion of treasures including the so-called giant from the Temple of Jupiter, a figure 7.65 metres high, and the early fifth-century BC statuette of a boy named Efebeo. Beyond is the astounding valley of the temples itself, whose perimeter extends to some 12 kilometres. Agrigento has again and again suffered minor earthquakes, which have brought down in ruins many of the ancient remains, but the effect is still overwhelming. Virtually every monument here dates from the sixth and fifth centuries BC. To the west stand the remains of the largest Doric temple to survive from antiquity, the Temple of Jupiter, measuring some 12 metres long by 56 metres wide. The original 'giant' is today sheltered in the archaeological museum, and the Atlas here is a copy. The temple

All that remains of the
Temple of Castor and Pollux,
Agrigento, built around
470 BC and re-erected
in 1836.

ruins in Goethe's time were, as he put it, 'scattered like the bones of a huge skeleton'.
Nineteenth-century archaeologists set it up again, as well as the four fallen columns and
pediment which today form a wistful corner of the former Temple of Castor and Pollux,
also known as the Temple of the Dioscuri. Massive stones lying on the ground trace the
former lineaments of this holy place.

Across the ravine from here are the two remaining columns of the Temple of Vulcan,
while along the spur, hidden among olive trees, stands the oldest temple of the valley,
that dedicated to Hercules. When – soon, I hope – the remaining columns and stones of
this temple are re-erected, it will be a majestic ruin, but nothing is likely to surpass the
magnificent Tempio della Concordia, which appears among the baths and cemeteries of
the villa area just beyond. This superbly preserved temple was built in 440 BC. Massy
steps rise to thirty-four columns of golden stone, which trace out a rectangle 42 metres

long by 20 metres wide; the decoration is simple and harmonious. 'Compared to Paestum,' said Goethe, 'it is the image of a god as opposed to the image of a giant.' The preservation of this pagan temple was the work of Christians, for in the fourth century it was transformed into a Christian basilica, dedicated to St Gregory, and continued in use until 1748.

A lonelier temple lies isolated along the *strada panoràmica* not far from the Greek walls of Agrigento. The Temple of Juno stood more or less intact from the fifth century BC until the Middle Ages, in spite of being partly destroyed by the Cartheginians in 406. You can, it is said, still find traces of the scorch marks left by their vandalism, but I cannot. Medieval earthquakes finally brought it low.

Although Agrigento had an Arab name for so long, it is hard, at least to my eyes, to detect a major Arabic influence on the architecture of the medieval city. The Christian renaissance in the eleventh century has by contrast left here several elegant Norman buildings, notably the eleventh-century cathedral of San Gerlando on the north side of the medieval quarter and the thirteenth-century abbey church of San Spirito. Founded in 1290, San Spirito is one of the loveliest abbeys in Sicily. As you enter the baroque interior of this church through its gothic doorway, the rose window and the double arcade force you to pause in admiration. Of the ancient abbey, the cloister, the chapter house and the refectory (today a library) have lost none of their original austerity.

The dramatist Luigi Pirandello, born here in 1867, lifted from Plato an epigram about his native city: 'In Agrigento people build as if they will never die and eat as if they have but an hour to live.' Something of the occasionally savage grandeur of Agrigento emerged in the playwright. Hating his domineering father, Pirandello poured into his plays resentment, iconoclasm and rebellion against unjustifiable rules. Audiences thrilled to his powerful, it seemed spiteful gift for denunciation. One of his favourite words was *schifo*, the Sicilian for an object that revolts a person's sensibilities, surely an expression he learned in his home town.

The successors of the Greeks, the shadowy Etruscans who dominated central Italy from the seventh to the fourth century BC, are not even granted by historians the use of their proper name. They called themselves Rasna or Rasena, the Greeks called them Tyrrhenians and the Romans gave them the name that has stuck, Tusci or Etrusci. The Greek historian Herodotus claimed that these people came from Asia Minor, and certainly their habit of burying their dead in *tumuli*, their language, and their Babylonian custom of divining the future from examining the livers of animals, might support his view. Equally plausibly, these resemblances between Etruscan and Babylonian civilizations might be explained simply by the fertile contacts of trade.

Their social structure was as sophisticated as was their art and their religion. By the end of the fifth century BC, most Etruscan cities had replaced kings with an oligarchy at the head of which presided a chief magistrate or *zilath*. Fascinated, preoccupied, entranced by and fearing the notion of life after death, they poured almost all their artistic brilliance into their funeral art, reserving what was left for the design and construction of monumentally superb cities. As early as the mid seventh century BC these cities stretched as far as the River Arno in northern Italy (including the whole of

The Temple of Juno at Agrigento rises above a terrain fissured by earthquakes.

present-day Tuscany) and as far as the Tiber in the south and east. By the next century the Etruscans had managed to fight their way into the Po valley and into Latium and Campania in the south. For over a hundred years from 616 BC, the Etruscan dynasty of the Tarquins ruled Rome itself. But their most evocative city in my view, and the one that preserves an aspect worthy of their powerful architecture, was Volterra, one of the twelve cities loosely joined together in an Etruscan federation based on Voltumna, near present-day Bolsena.

'The celebrated *Alabaster Works* of Volterra afford occupation to nearly two-thirds of the population,' observed the 1890 edition of Baedeker, 'but most of the patterns are unfortunately in very bad taste.' Either Baedeker was wrong or my own taste is execrable, for I relish the green and white alabaster chess sets, the amber necklaces and the lithe green figurines still produced by the traditional artists of Volterra. What Baedeker rightly observed is that, 'The traveller should visit the interesting work shops, where souvenirs may be purchased far more cheaply than at Florence or Leghorn.' The craftsmen of Volterra dub alabaster *la belva*, which means the wild beast, and those who mine it describe their profession as 'attacking the wild beast'. The deeper alabaster is mined, the finer its quality. Something in the region of a thousand skilled men in Volterra still sculpt and polish it, producing a fascinating variety of opalescent gems.

Along with the salt trade and the other mineral resources of Volterra, alabaster has supported the economy of the city since prehistory. Situated some sixty or so kilometres north-west of Siena, Volterra stands 550 metres above sea-level on one of the highest peaks of the mountain ridge that separates the valleys of the rivers Cecina and Era. I shall never forget the *frisson* I experienced after seeing what people here call the *balze*, the vertiginous, unstable cliffs from which Volterra rises. Only in the mid third century BC did Volterra surrender to Rome, joining the cities allied in a federation under her control. For over two years the walled city had withstood an assault by the forces of Sulla which began in 82 BC, before finally admitting defeat. Today the massive remains of the Etruscan walls form an outer ring to later defences dating from the thirteenth century. These Etruscan walls, whose remnants still retain their ancient grandeur, stretched around Volterra for 8 kilometres. The medieval walls are scarcely a third as long but nonetheless seem almost as powerful, rising to some 13 metres and in parts over 4 metres wide. The walls are pierced with gateways that have been frequently modified through the centuries, but the Porta all'Arco remains authentically Etruscan, not a trace of cement holding together the crumbling gray stones that support a beautifully turned Roman arch of harder, whiter stone. The Romans were respectful enough to retain three Etruscan sculptures of human heads in the rebuilding, their unwavering gaze welcoming the visitor back into the past. Do they represent Jupiter, Minerva and Juno, as some authorities claim? Their weather-worn features make it impossible for me to judge.

Via Porta all'Arco leads from this gateway to the heart of the town, Piazza dei Priori. As various monuments reveal, Volterra did not emerge triumphant from her wars with other great medieval cities. The fortress which the ruler of Florence, Lorenzo de'

The *balze*, the vertiginous, unstable cliffs on which Volterra is built.

Medici, built in the late fifteenth century, after the army of the Duke of Urbino had viciously subdued Volterra on Lorenzo's behalf, still towers over the city. Known as the Fortezza Nuova, it is notable for its five keeps, the middle one of which is called 'il Maschio' (the male) and today serves as a jail. Its partner is the fourteenth-century tower of the Fortezza Vecchia, which the Volterrans have dubbed 'la Femmina'.

Was it the forbidding aspect of this 'new' fortress that led D. H. Lawrence to describe the city as 'curiously isolated and grim'? Its altitude and exposed position have earned Volterra the soubriquet 'the windy city'. But in my eyes it is an underestimated gem, its architectural purity emphasized by the fact that nearly every major building was constructed out of the golden stone known as *la panchina*, from which is eventually derived alabaster itself. Occasional brick ornamentation relieves the general spare severity. Because the Florentines wished to keep Volterra permanently subservient, the Fortezza Nuova was the last great building constructed in the city.

The remains of Roman baths and an archaeological park separate Lorenzo de' Medici's Fortezza Nuova from the Piazza Martiri della Libertà. In 1909 the poet Gabriele d'Annunzio stayed in the Albergo Nationale in this piazza, and parts of a poem he composed there are inscribed on its wall. It brilliantly sums up the occasional eeriness of this remarkable city:

*Fondata nella rupe, alle tue porte*
*Senza stridore . . . ;*
*Il flagel della peste a dell guerra*
*Avea pigata e tronica la tua sorte*

Set upon crags, your gates
fail to screech . . . ;
The scourge of plague and the scourge of war,
warped and destroyed your destiny.

Reputed to be the oldest surviving Etruscan arch in Italy, the Porta all'Arco at Volterra incorporates three much eroded Etruscan heads.

The Piazza dei Priori itself lies in the midst of an austere, slightly threatening ensemble of buildings. Etruscan Volterra has for the moment been left behind. Not a single café or trattoria interrupts the beauty of the palaces here. The thirteenth-century Palazzo Pretorio flanks the eastern side of the square, its tower for some reason dubbed *il porcellino* (the piglet). Some say the nickname comes from a piglet carved on a corbel, though I have never made it out. What I do warm to is the deliberate irregularity of the arcades of its lower storey.

Opposite the Palazzo Pretorio rises Tuscany's oldest secular palace, the Palazzo dei Priori, which was built in the first half of the thirteenth century. Covering the façade are the coats of arms and escutcheons of the Florentine governors of the city, chased in terracotta and stone. The clock is set off-centre, over which rises a double-storeyed tower. Here too is Volterra's romanesque cathedral. Though it dates from the tenth century, some 300 years later Pisan masters remodelled its west façade and much else.

At the same time other Pisans were sculpting and painting the romanesque group of figures representing the Deposition which is now displayed in the north transept. The interior was altered again in 1584 by Leonardo Ricciarelli, the offspring of Daniele. The coffered ceiling, green, gold and blue, is painted with saintly heads. Ricciarelli, I think, stuccoed the columns to give the impression of granite.

Standing apart from the cathedral is the geometrically beautiful ensemble of its campanile of 1493 and the octagonal baptistery which Giroldo di Iacopo built in 1283 on the site of a pagan temple of the sun. Green and white marble sets off the baptistery's thirteenth-century doorway. Inside its a beautiful octagonal font, created by Andrea Sansovino at the very beginning of the sixteenth century and depicting not only the baptism of Jesus but also the four virtues.

Nearby is the diocesan museum of religious art, housed in Volterra's former episcopal palace, which once served as the city granary. Those tempted to pass by will miss seeing work by Antonio Pollaiuolo, a moving crucifixion which could have been created only by Giambologna, and Nicola Pisano's marble sculpture of the Madonna and Child. Here too is a somewhat cloying depiction of St Lino, son of Volterra, by Andrea della Robbia. According to dubious legend, this saint succeeded St Peter as pope around AD 67 and took the name Clement I. Like St Peter, he died a willing martyr for his faith. As the eighteenth-century hagiographer Alban Butler observed: 'How little are we acquainted with this spirit of fervour, charity, meekness, patience, and sincere humility.' These are the very virtues which della Robbia has captured.

Volterra has been the home of equally great men. A plaque in Via Roma marks the

LEFT
The Palazzo dei Priori, Volterra, is Italy's oldest surviving medieval palace.

RIGHT
A griffin seizes a goose: one of the coats of arms sculpted on Volterra's Palazzo Pretorio.

former home of Giordano Bruno, the Dominican monk who supported the view of Copernicus that the earth circles the sun against that of Aristotle who taught the opposite. This was a dangerous stance in the late sixteenth century. The doomed genius wrote exquisite poetry which sometimes seemed to presage his fate:

> *Al cor, al spirito, a l'alma*
> *non è piacer, o libertade, o vita,*
> *qual tanto arrida, giove e sa gradita,*
> *qual più sia dolce, graziosa ed alma,*
> *ch'il stento, giogo e morte,*
> *ch'ho per natura, voluntade e sorte*

> To my heart, my spirit, my soul
> no pleasure exists, or liberty or life
> that so much smiles upon, or serves, or is pleasant,
> that offers so much sweetness, grace and kindness,
> as the hardship, yoke and death
> which I accept by nature, will and fate.

He was burnt at the stake for heresy in Rome on 17 February 1600.

Twelfth and thirteenth-century houses, some of them equipped with towers, proliferate in this quarter of Volterra, the finest being the thirteenth-century Case-torri Buomparenti. Daniele da Volterra, the painter and sculptor, was born in *c*.1506 at no. 12 in the shady, curving Via Ricciarelli, a house noted for its low windows onto the street, apparently to allow children to peer through at passers-by. This road joins Via di San Lino, named after the martyr saint and pope who is claimed by Volterra as one of the godliest of her native sons. The present church dedicated to this Volterran pope was begun by Raffaele Maffei in 1480 and finished fifty years later.

Nearby are more enchanting medieval streets, sixteenth-century palaces and romanesque churches. Yet however much the Middle Ages and the era of the Renaissance make themselves felt in Volterra, the Etruscan epoch is never far away. Via G. Matteotti, the continuation of Via Guarnacci, is half of the Etruscan axis of Volterra (Etruscan town planning frequently involved a road cutting directly from one end of the city to the other). And an Etruscan museum virtually without parallel in Italy is situated nearby in Via Don Minzoni. The Museo Etrusco Guarnacci possesses a remarkable collection of some six hundred funeral urns, sculpted out of tufa, alabaster and terracotta. They date from the sixth to the first century BC and are frequently decorated with domestic scenes – people eating, a boy dancing – depicting life two millennia ago. Believing in a future life, the Etruscans could face even death with courage, and several of the lids of these urns show them peacefully breathing their last. The most widely known terracotta panel depicts an ancient married couple, stoically contemplating their end. Stories from Greek mythology – the death of Clytemnestra, Ulysses and the Sirens – decorate some of them. The museum also houses sculptures, ivories, armour, bronzes and coins which once adorned and were the commerce of the daily lives of the Romans.

To appreciate fully the Roman impact on Volterra you must stroll back to Via Guarnacci. It was laid out on the site of the former Roman forum, and beyond the city wall to the north-west are the breathtaking excavations of the Roman theatre which was built here in the first century before the birth of Jesus. Its orderly columns are both delicate and today functionless, save where they vainly try to raise the broken portico. The medieval gate here is known as the Porta Fiorentina (and also as the Porta di San Angelo). Those with a taste for more Etruscan remains should walk through it to follow Via Diana as far as the Porta Diana which is flanked on both sides by surviving parts of the city's Etruscan walls. To call on the judgment of the novelist Henry James, Volterra still preserves the mien of a 'small, shrunken, but still lordly prehistoric city'.

Today, Volterra is living on borrowed time. Through the Porta Menseri in the Etruscan walls you find yourself standing high above the astonishing *balze*. Inexorably the cliffs are approaching the city, and unless future scientists can stave off disaster, one day it will all tumble into dust. Some of it has already disappeared. As Gabriele d'Annunzio's vision of Volterra expressed it, 'I saw dead from your buried city.' Blithely the Volterrans have incised these words too on the wall of the Albergo Nationale in Piazza Martiri della Libertà.

D'Annunzio saw the skull beneath the skin. It is hard to judge whether the Etruscans were obsessed with death or whether they welcomed it as a release into some better life. Theirs was a complex religion, with a hierarchy of deities, each tier possessing different skills and powers. The possibility of life after death clearly inspired their funereal artists, whose sculptures and inscriptions, giving equal prominence to both husbands and wives, also reveal that men and women must have been accorded equal rights in Etruscan society. Their innermost secrets are undoubtedly sensed most strongly by visiting an Etruscan necropolis or two. Some of the finest of their tombs, in which the imagined future life of the Etruscans reflects their lives in this world, are grouped outside the hilltown of Cerveteri, which lies 74 kilometres from Rome in the foothills of the Ceriti mountains. An ensemble of circular *tumuli* marks the Etruscan graves dug out of the tufa.

Part of Volterra's Roman amphitheatre.

Cerveteri, whose very fortifications jut from Etruscan foundations, was founded in the eighth century BC. Today the hilltown is also blessed with the partly romanesque church of Santa Maria (whose treasure is a painting of 1471 by Lorenzo di Viterbo), a medieval *rocca* and the sixteenth-century Palazzo Ruspoli, now an archaeological museum, while the neighbourhood is known for its artichokes. But Cerveteri's chief claim to fame is its Etruscan necropolis.

Lying outside the present-day city, some 2 kilometres north-west, this is truly a town of the dead, with streets and squares linking the remarkably complex tombs, some shaped like beehives, others substantial stone houses, others simple grottoes hewn to receive cremated ashes. The vast tomb known today as La Banditaccia is beautifully situated amidst pines and cypresses. Even though this is a place of the departed, the daily life of Etruscan men and women is depicted in their immaculate carvings, especially their love of games. Animals sport amongst humans. The fourth-century BC tomb of the reliefs is justly famous for its coloured stucco-work.

> They are dead, with all their vices,
> And all that is left
> Is the shadowy monomania of some cypresses
> And tombs.

wrote D. H. Lawrence. These Etruscans live on in heroic legend, especially their king, Lars Porsena. In 508 BC he even dared besiege Rome itself, an act immortalized in Thomas Babington Macaulay's *Lays of Ancient Rome*.

> Lars Porsena of Clusium
> By the nine gods he swore
> That the great house of Tarquin
> Should suffer wrong no more.
> By the Nine Gods he swore it,
> And named a trysting day,
> And bade his messengers ride forth,
> East and west and south and north,
> To summon his array.

At the end of the sixth century BC Lars Porsena was king of one of the most important towns of Etruria, known by the Etruscans as Chamars and by the Romans as Clusium. Modern Chiusi lies just off the Autostrada del Sole south of the lake of the same name. A romanesque cathedral now dominates the old centre, but as you peer more closely at its

LEFT
An ancient doorway at Cerveteri.

RIGHT
The Tomba dei Capitelli at Cerveteri is hewn straight from the existing rock.

pillars you perceive that the architect cannibalized the Roman and Etruscan remains of a pagan temple. Some architectural historians insist that nearly all of it was built from Etruscan stones. To the left of the cathedral stands the National Etruscan Museum. Jewellery, alabaster and terracotta sarcophagi, and funeral urns (some of them delicately painted in glowing colours) are housed here, excavated from the massive Etruscan necropolis in the surrounding countryside. The most famous sarcophagus depicts Gauls fighting and a dead Etruscan named Lars Sententinus.

Fired by these riches, buy a ticket at the museum and make the short trip north of Chiusi to visit at least one of the excavated tombs which the Etruscans dug in the tufa outside the town. Although the frescoes on many of the funeral urns are severely decayed, some of them retain their lively scenes of dancers, while wall-paintings depict wrestlers and athletes. Etruscan labyrinths pierce almost the whole of ancient Chiusi, and beside these evocative remains of a past civilization, the cathedral, the ruins of the twelfth-century *fortezza* and the fourteenth-century church of San Francesco fade into virtual obscurity. So labyrinthine are the Etruscan galleries that one wonders why fissures do not swallow up the town. Twentieth-century Italians still make their homes in the tunnels underneath the modern city.

Lars Porsena is said by Pliny to have built himself a tomb at Chiusi 100 metres long and 20 metres high. No-one has ever discovered this tomb, but many more have been found here. The Tomba della Scimmia (Tomb of the She-ape) has burial chambers decorated with wildly animated wall-paintings of animals, naked youths, dancers and gorgons. The Tomba della Pellegrina, from the third century BC, is almost as fine.

Chiusi is still recognizably an Etruscan hilltown. Elsewhere in Italy the appearance of similarly important Etruscan towns has often been overlaid by later buildings, and you must seek more determinedly for Etruscan remains. As you climb through the vineyards and olives up to Montalcino, 41 kilometres south of Siena, the six gates of the thirteenth-century walls surrounding the town, its medieval and arcaded Palazzo Comunale and the romanesque church of Sant'Agostino (blessed with fourteenth-century frescoes) could allow anyone to forget that the Etruscans, followed by the Romans, once prospered here. Paintings by Bartolo di Fredi grace the civic museum (his finest works here, in my view, are a *Deposition* of 1382 and a *Coronation of the Virgin* of 1388), and even when you reach the prehistoric and Etruscan remains of the Archaeological Museum you find them housed in a room decorated by the early sixteenth-century Sienese artist Sodoma. Yet the Etruscans seized on this little spot, a hill rising 567 metres above the valleys of the Arbia, Orcia and Ombrone, as an ideal site for one of their fortified towns.

Magliano in Toscana similarly conceals its ancient origins at first. This Tuscan town, situated on the Roman Aurelian way 11 kilometres north-east of Orbetello, still boasts medieval ramparts, a couple of romanesque churches which were much embellished in later centuries, and the Palazzo dei Priori built in 1430. Nonetheless, its Etruscan credentials are warranted by the massive necropolis $2\frac{1}{2}$ kilometres south-east, close by a ruined romanesque church dedicated to St Bruzio. Umbrian Bettona, by contrast, beautifully situated on an olive-crowned hill some 20 kilometres south-east

of Perugia, instantly proclaims its antiquity by the remains of the Etruscan walls surrounding its thirteenth-century heart (the churches of Santa Maria Maggiore and San Crispolto, and the Palazzo del Podestà). Forty metres of massive, irregular blocks of stone survive from the defences of ancient Bettona, as does a well dug by the same Etruscans who twenty-five centuries ago fortified this crumbling town.

One Etrusco-Roman hilltown which today lies completely open to the elements, overlaid by scarcely a single later building, is Tuscolo. A well signposted road to Tuscolo winds picturesquely up from Frascati, 18 kilometres south-east of Rome. On the way another charming hill-town appears on a wooded hill across the valley to the left as the road emerges from some trees. This is Monte Porzio Catone, which allegedly derives its name from the celebrated Roman citizen Marcus Porcius Cato, who was born in a little hamlet on the slopes of Tuscolo in 234 BC. A soldier who fought for the Romans against Hannibal, and already famous in his late teens, Cato rose rapidly until he was appointed consul and finally censor, one of the magistrates who supervised the public morals of the people. A determined opponent of Rome's enemies, above all the hated Carthage, and also of the lax morals of her citizens, this incorruptible man wrote the oldest piece of Latin prose that still survives, a treatise on farming called *De Agri Cultura*. Alas for Monte Porzio Catone, some scholars deny any connection between the hilltown and this great man, alleging that it derives its name from another Cato, tutor of the son of a self-indulgent Roman general named Lucullus whose villa once stood nearby.

Whatever the truth, Roman Monte Porzio Catone has been virtually swallowed up by the medieval walls, the sixteenth-century Palazzo Borghese and, in the same piazza, the church of Santissimi Gregorio e Antonio, which was built at the end of the fifteenth century and greatly remodelled by Girolamo Rainaldi in 1666. The Borghese family were reputed to be exceedingly rich, and one of them, a cardinal of the Catholic church, took up residence in the *palazzo* in 1613. Yet today this building, with its rows of unadorned rectangular and square windows, seems a quiet, unprepossessing affair – apart from the main archway surmounted by a balcony – with haphazard metal clamps along the walls giving it a poverty-stricken air.

Ancient Tuscolo, a couple of kilometres south of Monte Porzio Catone, has by no means been engulfed by later ages. Instead her medieval accretions were swept away. Here ten centuries or so before the birth of Jesus a city was founded, legend has it by Telegonus, son of Ulysses by the goddess Circe, the bewitching enchantress who transformed all those who drank her potion into swine. The Roman chronicler Festus took a soberer view and attributed the foundation of Tusculum (as it was then called, and still is by some) to the Etruscans. Soon, however, the religion of the Greeks triumphed on this hill. The summit, as its archaeological remains reveal, was fortified and at least two temples were built there, one dedicated to Jove, the other to Castor and Pollux. Meanwhile Tuscolo was developing into one of the leading cities in central Italy, and the Romans managed to subdue her only in the fifth century, when she fell to the army of Tarquinius Superbus's son-in-law, Octavius Mamilius.

The peace treaty decreed that the Romans and the Tuscolans were to regard each other as equals, ready with mutual aid. In 381 BC the Tuscolans broke their agreement, siding disastrously with the Volsci, the warlike people who dominated Latium until the Romans subdued them in the fourth century BC. Yet a year later they were accepted as Roman citizens and thenceforth provided the city with some of its most distinguished officials and noble families. Tuscolo came to its cruel end only in the Middle Ages, after a family named Teofilatti became Counts of Tuscolo. In 1167 they managed to defeat the papal forces outside Monte Porzio Catone. In 1191 Pope Celestine III took his revenge by destroying the fortifications that protected the stronghold of his enemy. Now Tuscolo was doomed. Rome invaded again in 1195, and six years later the pope agreed to crown Henry IV as Holy Roman Emperor only if he would raze the town.

These stirring events seem utterly at odds with the peaceful aspect of Tuscolo today. You wind on through the trees to reach an ample parking spot some five minutes' walk from the top of the hill. The path emerges into the open to offer a panorama of the wooded Alban hills and the cultivated valley below, before reaching a Roman amphitheatre which once seated 3000 spectators. An ellipse measuring 80 by 50 metres, its elegance is enhanced by the particular skill with which the stone blocks have been set diagonally in the walls, a technique known as *opus reticulatum* since it gives the effect of stone netting. Those who built it carved their masons' marks on the blocks, enabling us to date the amphitheatre as having been built in the second century AD.

Even before the construction of the amphitheatre, this spot evidently charmed the Emperor Tiberius (42 BC–AD 37), for he decided to make it his home when he left Capri to live with the widow of his brother Drusus. By now rich Romans looked uponTuscolo as a cool suburb where a villa afforded a welcome retreat from their humid capital. The arches and ruins at the eastern end of the amphitheatre are from Tiberius's villa.

We owe the initial excavation of Tuscolo to the patronage of Lucien Bonaparte, Napoleon's younger brother, who had been created Prince of Canino by the Pope. He lived in the sixteenth-century Villa Ruffinella, just outside Frascati on the road to Tuscolo. One day, perhaps, modern archaeologists will uncover for us the palace of the military commander which was built on this hill, as well as the remains of the numerous other villas which lie buried here, including (it is believed) that in which Cicero delivered his orations published as the *Tuscolanae Disputationes*. Till then there is much from the past to enjoy. A narrow, flagged and leafy road (Via Tuscolana Antica) leads – as it has done for possibly two millennia – up to yet another theatre, half the size of the one we have just seen and retaining its director's stall, the actors' rooms behind the stage and enough pillars to enable visitors to imagine themselves at a performance in the first century BC, when it was built. Behind the theatre is the reservoir or *piscina* which once supplied the baths of Roman Tuscolo.

The northern summit of Tuscolo is marked by a massive cross. Here you can explore the ruins of a medieval fortress and gaze across the plains of Latium which lie over 600 metres below. Over to the right are Monte Porzio Catone and Camaldoli; to the left rises Monte Cavo, as well as the hilltowns of Castelgandolfo and Grottoferrata (see pp. 198–200 and 180–2); and if you look towards the sea you can spot the dome of St Peter's, Rome.

Rising on a spur of Monte Prenestini 38 kilometres outside that city is the ancient town of Palestrina. Modern Palestrina lies in fact at the foot of the hill. Steeply terraced slopes climb to what initially appears to be a medieval village, fortified with a double ring of walls and entered by two medieval gates. The fact that this was in 1525 the birthplace of the celebrated composer Giovanni Pierluigi da Palestrina serves to reinforce the notion that we are about to visit a remnant of the Middle Ages; but as the former name of Palestrina, Praeneste, indicates, the town is much older and indeed stands on pre-Roman foundations.

The bombs of World War II helped to uncover them, though excavations had begun a couple of decades earlier. Today Palestrina's proudest monument is the beautifully excavated temple of Fortuna Primigenia, which was built in the second century BC. But Palestrina itself existed at least as far back as the eighth century BC. At the beginning of

At Palestrina, the superb stairway of the Roman Temple of Fortuna Primigenia rises to the Palazzo Barberini.

the fifth century, her leaders decided to throw in their lot with the Romans. Their most costly decision was to side with the Roman general and consul Marius during the civil war which began in 88 BC, provoked by Marius's intense envy of the power and prestige of his rival, the general and statesman Sulla. Sulla took his revenge in 81 BC; Palestrina was razed and its citizens put to the sword. Only the temple escaped destruction. Sulla was a man who respected the gods, and the Temple of Fortuna Primigenia was famed throughout his realms for its priestesses' powers of divination. Instead of destroying it, he restored and enriched the holy place. Four terraces slope down for almost 200 metres, encompassing ancient shrines, basilicas and arches.

The semicircular arcade which embraces this temple now also delimits the Palazzo Barberini, for the architects who first designed it in the eleventh century respected their Roman past. A building of considerable charm, its present aspect derives chiefly from a rebuilding of 1493 and a further reconstruction in the mid seventeenth century. Warm russet walls rise above ancient masonry. A double row of simple square windows does not distract from the graceful curve of the façade, while a renaissance balustrade in white stone enlivens the flight of steps leading up to the entrance. It takes more than a moment to realize that the boutiques below are inserted in the stones of what was once a pagan temple.

The *palazzo* is today the home of the Praenestine Archaeological Museum. Alongside the many fragments of sculpture and sophisticatedly engraved bronze mirrors on display is a fabled treasure: a shimmering polychrome mosaic, dating from the first century BC and depicting the inundation of the River Nile and a remarkable vision of the whole of Egypt. A fascination with the flooding Nile permeated the imagination of Italians in the first century BC. They were inspired by the mosaics of Alexandria, of which this is one of the finest extant examples (though some scholars insist that it is a Roman copy based on an Alexandrian design). Among the funeral busts and Roman sculptures also housed here is part of a huge statue of Fortuna, said to have been sculpted in the second century BC. The interior of the *palazzo*, frescoed in the seventeenth century by the Zuccari brothers, is a treat.

Past a fifteenth-century Franciscan convent you reach the cathedral of Sant'Agapito, whose romanesque campanile was rebuilt in the twelfth century. Here again the Middle Ages rest on the Roman era. The cathedral rises on the site of the Temple of Juno, which stood here from the third century BC, while the Piazza Margherita which is now the cathedral square was laid out on what was once the forum. Underneath the cathedral is the oracle which so impressed the general. A gateway beside the adjoining former seminary leads to further riches of the Roman era, the vast terraces and sacred buildings of the *area sacra*, and the sacred grotto, the Antro delle Sorti (south-east of the cathedral), whose mosaic pavement, dating from the first century BC, depicts the bed of the sea.

Palestrina once boasted its own acropolis, lying 4 kilometres north of the city of Castel San Pietro Romano. Its polygonal walls are still intact. Signposted from the crossroads north of the Palazzo Barberini, the site, 752 metres above sea-level, is worth visiting for its ruined *rocca* and panorama alone. When it rains here – as can happen torrentially in a thunderstorm – water jets exhilaratingly through the specially-bored holes in the city walls.

As one might expect, the region surrounding ancient Rome boasts a number of other hilltowns displaying precisely this pattern of medieval and renaissance streets and buildings superimposed on an Etruscan or Roman town. Historians insist that Sutri, whose name derives from Saturn, was founded even earlier than Etruscan times by a tribe known as the Pelasgi. If so, there are no architectural remains from this ancient people, but the coiling medieval streets of Sutri are still surrounded by red Etruscan walls which set off the white stone of a mighty Roman arch. They rise sheer from the rock, merging into houses above and pressing down on troglodyte caves below.

The central Piazza del Comune with its dolphin fountain momentarily forsakes the Etrusco-Roman period, but Etruscan remains and Roman heads are set in the wall of

This mosaic depicting the Nile in flood, dating from the first century BC, is displayed in the Palazzo Barberini at Palestrina.

the archway leading into the courtyard of the classical Municipio. In the courtyard itself an ancient sarcophagus is now used as a drinking trough. Similarly, the fountain in the piazza has largely lost its original function. However drab, such fountains were once an essential element in any hilltown. As the historian Christopher Brooke observed, 'It is exceedingly inconvenient to live on a hilltop, especially before modern methods of water supply were devised. Even if it be true that the Roman system of water supply survived in Perugia and a few other cities into the Middle Ages and has been believed to be better than anything the modern world has yet provided – in most places water was hard to come by and almost as expensive at times as wine.'

The charm of the piazza is eclipsed by the splendour of Sutri's oval Etrusco-Roman amphitheatre, dug out of tufa. Those with a taste for archaeology should apply to the local tourist office to visit the site, which lies along the Via Cassia in the direction of Rome. Those with a nose for the continuities of religion should seek out the Villa Staderini, where the church of the Madonna del Prato rises on the site of an Etruscan tomb and still boasts fragments of Etruscan frescoes.

Nowhere does it become clearer how the evocative curves of an ancient amphitheatre can dominate the atmosphere of an Italian hilltown than in Fiesole above Florence. Inhabited in the Bronze Age and settled by the Etruscans 700 years before the Christian era, for centuries the town played a crucial role in protecting the trading arteries of ancient Italy. When they took the town in 80 BC, the Romans dubbed it Faesulae. Ancient Fiesole is still only partly overlaid by later buildings, and you can today make out all the trappings of an Etruscan and Roman town. Where you alight from the bus from Florence, in the Piazza Mino da Fiesole, you are treading the Roman forum.

The cathedral brings one out of Etruria into the Middle Ages. Its battlemented campanile of 1213 is notable in a land of magical belfries chiefly because it is a landmark visible from far around. Walk inside the building if only to see the mid fifteenth-century triptych by Bicci di Lorenzo on the high altar and Mino da Fiesole's sculptures in the capella Salutati (which include the mid fourteenth-century tomb of Bishop Salutati). Then the age of the Etruscans and Romans reappears. Even the garden of the nearby late seventeenth-century bishop's palace abuts onto fragments of Etruscan wall. Walk around the cathedral apse and you immediately reach the open-air Roman theatre. It seems odd that its existence remained forgotten until 1809. Today it is not only beautifully excavated but also returns to its original purpose in July and August during the Estate Fiesolana, Florence's summer festival. This amphitheatre dates from the first century BC, though it was subsequently considerably enlarged and now seats 3000 spectators. The baths nearby, first constructed in the century before the birth of Jesus, were likewise enlarged, under the Emperor Hadrian. Here too is a museum of Etruscan and Roman remains full of the steles, tombs, statues and busts of the people who walked Fiesole in antiquity. The museum, though built after World War I, itself resembles a Roman temple.

Fiesole displays once again the phenomenon seen throughout the West: a Christian church built on a pagan foundation. From the cathedral square Via San Francesco climbs steeply upwards to the church of Sant'Allessandro, whose site was once occupied by a Roman temple of Bacchus and before that by an Etruscan temple. The Christians who built it in the seventh century had no scruples about incorporating the old Roman columns in their new church. Today it is much changed, though the ancient columns remain.

Fiesole is but one of many Italian hilltowns whose antiquity has refused to be buried by the achievements of later ages. One of the Castelli Romani, Albano Laziale, scarcely seems a hilltown at first sight, for you approach it from Ariccia across a viaduct built over the deep Ariccia ravine in 1843, a gift of the Pope. The road passes the twelfth-century church of San Pietro on the left, built of stones cannibalised from former Roman buildings. Then the impressive ruins of the Porta Pretoria appear, built in the second and third centuries AD. Once again these ancient remains were uncovered by the bombs of World War II.

Not surprisingly, the church of Santa Maria della Rotunda in via Saffi, with its fifteenth-century frescoes and an eighth-century byzantine Madonna, and the town hall are both built on the sites of Roman villas, while the Cisternone in the same street as Santa Maria della Rotunda is a swimming pool that still welcomes bathers after 2000 years of existence. Finally, there is the ruined amphitheatre of Septimus Severus (146–211), reached by a steep road that winds uphill from the corner of Piazza San Paolo in the direction of Castelgandolfo.

All these hilltowns and cities remain remarkably unblemished by the centuries. The same cannot be said of Taormina in Sicily. Although the American historian Henry Adams judged that Taormina was one of the most beautiful spots in the world, it has coped with the press of tourists only by constructing a massive underground car park. Yet nothing can spoil its vistas, for the town rises high above the Ionian Sea. In the impressive remains of an ancient Greek and Roman amphitheatre (after that at Syracuse, the largest in Sicily), Roman columns frame views of the water and of Mount Etna across the bay, while the tiers of the amphitheatre shut out the rest of the town. An annual music festival is held here, when the ruins resound with Verdi's *Les vêpres siciliennes*, Mascagni's *Cavalleria rusticana* and Puccini's *Turandot*. D. H. Lawrence lived at Taormina in the 1920s, and a plaque identifies his former home. 'Ah, dark garden, dark garden,' he wrote in *Sea and Sardinia*, 'with your olives and your wine, your medlars and mulberries and many almond trees, your steep terraces ledged high above the sea.' In spite of tourism, he would still, I think, praise the place.

But my favourite among all these ancient hilltowns is fierce Tarquinia, 93 kilometres north of Rome. Tarquinia always seems to me a delightful backwater, strange and eerie, with its white walls rising above white rocks pitted with cracks and caves, designed, I think, to keep out the twentieth century. Its alleged founder was Tarchon, brother (or maybe son) of the Lydian prince Tyrrhenus, who gave his name to the sea across a strip of fertile plain as flat as a haddock. Tarquinia was numbered among the twelve great Etruscan cities, and legend has it that here Tages, the son of Hercules, taught the Etrucans the skills of divination and soothsaying, skills which their later Roman masters so much prized.

As a child, Tages was dug out of the earth by a ploughman, who was all the more

Medieval Tarquinia rises over the site of the former Etruscan necropolis.

38

startled to discover that the clay-covered infant had the wisdom of an old man. The ploughman brought Tages to the people of Tarquinia. 'The crowd listened as he spoke of many subjects,' wrote Cicero, 'and they collected and wrote down all he said'. Their laws, as well as their ability to read the future from the entrails of animals, came from this divine source. Tarquin the Proud, who ruled Rome in the second half of the sixth century BC, almost certainly came from here. Disgraced by his vicious attack on the virtue of Lucretia (as Shakespeare put it, an earthly saint seduced by a devil who was 'bewitch'd by lust's foul charm'), Tarquin was forced into exile. In the words of Shakespeare's inspired doggerel, the noble Romans decided on his punishment and:

> When they had sworn to this advised doom,
> They did conclude to bear dead Lucrece thence,
> To show her bleeding body thorough Rome,
> And so to punish Tarquin's foul offence:
> Which being done with speedy diligence,
> The Romans plausibly did give consent
> To Tarquin's everlasting banishment.

At this time Tarquinia did not stand on its present hill, but stretched along the plain to the sea. The hill on which the present city rises served only as Tarquinia's necropolis. So everything remained until the sixth century AD, when the Saracens devastated the city. The citizens fled to their necropolis, which for the next thirteen centuries they called Corneto. Tarquinia only assumed the name of the ancient Etruscan city in 1922.

If the Etruscan necropolis marks the earliest surviving monument of Tarquinia, one of the latest of its architectural masterpieces is encountered immediately you enter the city. Palazzo Vitelleschi in Piazza Cavour was built between 1436 and 1439 for the warlike cleric Cardinal Giovanni Vitelleschi. The cardinal did not enjoy his new home for long. Accused of treachery in 1440, he was seized and executed in Castello Sant'Angelo on the orders of Pope Eugenius IV.

His palace remains unfinished, yet the contrast between the decorative frills of the windows, with their twisting columns, and the sobriety of the bare, fortress-like stone walls of the rest of the building is entirely agreeable. The cardinal's architects incorporated in his palace several older buildings, whose oddities combine in a surprisingly successful amalgam. Palazzo Vitelleschi is now the Museo Nazionale Tarquiniense, where visitors plunge back into Tarquinian history. No fewer than sixty painted Etruscan tombs have been found in the neighbourhood, and the museum has much profited from them. Sarcophagi and sculpture dating from at least the sixth century BC are ranged in the arcades of its courtyard, which is surmounted by gothic galleries. Half reclining on their tombs, these sculpted Etruscan ancients peacefully await the next world, where they expected at least a shadowy existence. The first-floor gallery is filled with finds excavated from the necropolis. Amphora and cups frequently carved with the figure of Dionysius, the Greek God of nature, merriment and wine, remind us that the Etruscans were revellers as well as soothsayers. Sculptures of Hercules and Apollo point to the Greek influence on their art. The loveliness of these works in no way prepares you for the splendid winged horses in the next room, dating from the third century BC and dug up from the ancient city. As you wander on through the galleries, ancient paintings reveal the Etruscans banqueting or their elegant youths indulging in games. Much later in date but just as arresting is Filippo Lippi's *Madonna and Child* in the palace chapel, painted in the first half of the fifteenth century.

For a moment medieval Tarquinia interrupts one's survey of its antiquities. Via Mazzini passes the bust of the nineteenth-century patriot after whom the street is named and runs alongside the walls of the Palazzo Vitelleschi, rebuilt after a fire in 1642. The *palazzo* stands beside one of the eighteen medieval towers that survive from many more which once studded this city. The present *duomo* was built two hundred years or so after the palazzo, though its apse is fifteenth century and its façade a modern reconstruction incorporating some ill-preserved decorative stone and glass inlay signed by Pietro di Ranuccio Romano in 1143. The frescoes of the apse were painted by Antonio da Viterbo in 1508. I warm to its classical organ, which dates from 1882.

This cathedral is lovely; but its elegance seems to me utterly out of place in the medieval quarter of this ancient city. I scarcely linger here, but like a hungry dog hasten up Via di Porta Castello to reach a much more delightful church. Santa Maria di Castello stands beside the romantic eleventh-century curtain wall of the former castle of Tarquinia. The church was built a century later, a delicious blend of romanesque, gothic and Lombardic elements reminiscent of Ancona cathedral (see pp. 190–4). Its sparse mosaic decoration dates from 1143, the year when Pietro di Ranuccio Romano built the beautiful central porch. Holes let into the brickwork still await the supports of a never-added marble façade. Over the protruding doorway to the left, the brickwork changes in order to support a double-arched belfry in which, oddly enough, hang no bells. Inside the church the capitals are simple and delicate, the gleaming red and green pavement mosaics entrancing, and Giovanni di Guittone's polychrome marble pulpit of 1209 powerfully impressive. A rose window pierces the north wall.

No fewer than three thirteenth-century churches – San Pancrazio, San Martino and Santissima Annunziata – doze in the crumbling medieval quarter of Tarquinia. On the way to them, in Piazza Giacomo Matteotti, rise a pretty baroque fountain and the partly romanesque Palazzo Municipale, its three towers, all that remain of the original eight, heralding the more fortified aspect of the older houses. This quarter of Tarquinia also shelters the thirteenth-century Palazzo dei Priori, which boasts no fewer than four towers. Via del Torri here is hemmed in with fragmented towers. Though its houses are almost as tumbledown, people live in them.

These citizens no longer worship in their medieval churches. Today neither San Pancrazio nor Santissima Annunziata attracts any congregation. San Salvatore is equally deserted, and the bells of its campanile are no longer rung. Just beyond it, superbly sited on the edge of the cliff, San Giacomo has been totally abandoned. The utterly haphazard façade of San Martino displays alarming cracks.

Indeed, the Etruscan necropolis itself seems more alive than some of these churches. For over 400 years, from the sixth to the second century BC, the Etruscans filled some of the homes of their dead with the most vivid paintings. Not all of them are open to

A baroque fountain drips gently in Piazza Giacomo Matteotti, Tarquinia.

visitors (and few of us would have the stamina to explore nearly 6000 excavated tombs, or even the sixty or so that are painted). The paintings show ruddy-faced men and slender, whiter women, banqueting as they face death. In others, people hunt boars, watch prisoners and slaves doing battle with fierce beasts and contemplate Hercules blinding Polyphemus (one of the mythological stories the Etruscans learned from the Greeks). Even the nether regions themselves are inhabited by old friends: Pluto, Proserpine, Tiresias, Agamemnon, Theseus and the rest. Whereas most Etruscan art, such as that at Chiusi, is painted in black and a brownish-purple against a background of whitened terracotta, the artists at Tarquinia relished blues and greens as well. Their subjects were also more adventurous. And they clearly enormously enjoyed the fact that their superb hilltown overlooked the sea. One of the tombs depicts boys on the shore, slinging stones at birds and diving from the rocks into the water.

# 2

# THE MIGHT AND GRACE
# OF ROMANESQUE

O F ALL THE CONQUESTS of the Normans, that of southern Italy and Sicily is probably the least appreciated and certainly the most intriguing, a conquest achieved not by princes and kings but by lesser knights who – according to their chronicler Amatus of Montecassino – rode on horseback through meadows and gardens, 'happily cavorting hither and thither'. At the end of the tenth century, returning from Jerusalem, a group of Norman pilgrims were the first to come upon this beautiful and often spectacular part of Italy. Later chroniclers would perceive their conquest of these realms as analogous with the Crusades themselves, for the enemies of the Normans here were Moslem Arabs. When Duke Robert Guiscard of Normandy led a force of 700 northmen against twice that number of Moslems in the mid eleventh century, before the battle he quoted to his troops a text from the Gospel of St Matthew: 'Be not afraid, for we have Jesus Christ with us, who says, "If you have the faith of a grain of mustard seed, you shall say to this mountain, remove hence to yonder place; and it shall remove, and nothing shall be impossible to you."'

Count Roger d'Hauteville had begun the Norman conquest of Sicily in the second half of the twelfth century, and after Palermo fell to the Normans in 1072, Guiscard created him Count of Sicily. The Norman rulers prospered here, and also absorbed the arts of those they had conquered. Initially Moslem models served for their secular buildings, their castles and palaces. When it came to religious architecture, at times the Normans built churches with Moorish domes, and eventually they created the unique Sicilian romanesque, with its gently pointing arches. In 1174 the Norman King William II decided to build a sepulchral church for himself and his family. His chosen spot lay not in France, but on a hill overlooking Palermo, by now capital not just of southern Italy but of a kingdom that stretched into Greece. He summoned architects and artists from virtually every corner of the Norman empire. All of them were skilled in the first form of architecture ever to achieve any sort of international currency, that massive, non-naturalistic and often dazzlingly distorted style which nineteenth-century architectural historians dubbed 'romanesque', a style which was based in part on Roman patterns but also included elements from the Orient. The Normans clearly relished the rhythms created by a succession of piers and columns. Work on William's great church began in 1176, on a terrace dominating the valleys of the Oreto and the Conca d'Oro some 8 kilometres south-west of Palermo. Within six years the embryo sepulchre was advanced enough to serve an archbishop as his cathedral church.

The Norman empire by now stretched into the Byzantine world (the region which had constituted the eastern half of the Roman empire), and the romanesque cathedral of Santa Maria la Nuova at Monreale exudes an aura of Byzantium as well as a suggestion of Saracen architecture. Yet some of its most celebrated artists were Tuscans. In 1186 Bonanno da Pisa came from his native city to fashion the superb bronze doors at the west end which are now sheltered by an elaborately decorated seventeenth-century porch. Their forty sculpted panels are devoted to scenes from the Old and New Testaments, and if you cannot read the inscriptions this is because they are in the almost forgotten Sicilian language. On the north side a sixteenth-century portico guards a mosaic frieze as well as another bronze door, this one created by Barisano da Trani around the year 1190 and incorporating twenty-eight panels sculpted with saints. Such details subsume themselves under the breathtakingly simple overall conception of what is undoubtedly the finest Norman church in Sicily and one of the romanesque marvels of the Middle Ages. That diverse styles have somehow been brought together into a unity is evinced as you walk round the church. Decoration helps to hold them together. Interlacing arches of the black lava that is abundant in Sicily and pale orange limestone decorate both the west façade (one of whose two towers is still unfinished) and the apse, the arches pierced with numerous rose windows. There are in fact three apses; two smaller ones aligned with the aisles of the basilica flank the great easternmost one.

The interior gleams with Byzantine-style mosaic, gold-leaf glinting amongst the brilliant colours of the polished stones. No seats clutter the cathedral's spaciousness or conceal its marble, porphyry and granite patterned floor. The pillars, capitals and arches unfold towards the east end. On the high, gently-pointed arch which announces the apse, two angels bless the high altar. On the apse, Christ Pantocrator blesses us in return. The altar itself is stepped up – though I doubt it was at the consecration in 1182 – but not so much as to spoil the spiritual sweep of the building.

Then you spot the patterned decorations on the underside of the slightly pointed, Arabic-style arches (another curiosity of Sicilian romanesque, for elsewhere the Normans built round arches), and after that the fact that the ceiling is still made of wood. Thanks to the subsequent economic decline of this part of Italy, there was no attempt to replace it with something more elaborate in stone. Even after a fire of 1811 the Sicilians wisely restored their wooden roof, instead of replacing it. At the east end, under the figure of Jesus, is the enthroned Madonna to whom this cathedral is dedicated. She is attended by angels and apostles and sits above a group of saints. An urn on the high altar contains the heart of King Louis the Pious of France, who died of the plague at Tunis in 1270. To the right, above the episcopal throne, the founder offers his church to the Blessed Virgin. To the left, above the royal throne, he receives in return his crown from Jesus. On the right of the apse the English archbishop Thomas Becket is depicted in glory. William II's father-in-law had done penance for his complicity in the murder of the saint, and the Normans were here acknowledging (in theory at least) the supremacy of the spiritual over the lay power.

But the church is memorable above all for the cycle of some 130 romanesque mosaics. Begun in 1182 and finished (probably by Venetian craftsmen) in the early

The interlacing limestone and lava arches of Monreale cathedral.

thirteenth century, these depict the story of salvation, from the creation of the world to the triumph of the church. They wind around the cathedral, running down the south side of the nave across the west wall and back down the north side. More mosaics in the aisles illustrate the teachings of Jesus, while chapels here house the tombs of prominent Normans: the porphyry sarcophagus of William I, who died in 1166; the white marble tomb of William II, which was created in 1575 though he died in 1190; and the tombs of William I's wife Margaret and of his sons Roger and Henry. The only intrusion into this cool romanesque masterpiece is the baroque Chapel of the Crucifixion.

The beauty of the twelfth-century cloisters of the Benedictine monastery which once adjoined this cathedral rivals that of the great church itself. Somehow the architects managed to vary the designs of the twin columns and arches of these cloisters without disturbing the atmosphere of peace. The arches again are slightly pointed. The capitals are full of the imagery and imagination of western medieval art. Naked men scramble amid foliage as large as themselves; a man vigorously stabs a bull; delicate tracery surrounds a carving of William II offering his cathedral to the Madonna (a helpful angel helping him to carry a scale model of the building); the angel Gabriel, sword erect, brusquely announces to Mary that she is to bear the Son of God, while she recoils aghast; a couple of massive lizards seem about to bite the ears off a poor human. The twelfth-century architects of the cloister also provided it with an exquisite fountain. And here, as on the exterior of the cathedral, they utilized an interlaced pattern of lava and limestone. From this cloister there is a view of the cathedral's north tower, its unfaced walls blank, simple and satisfying.

Monreale, the city that grew up around the great cathedral, was an exceptional phenomenon, for the Normans in Sicily conquered a land that had cradled civilizations from antiquity. Generally they had no need to found new settlements, but simply took over ancient towns and cities and adapted them to their own needs. You can see similarly exotic elements in the romanesque buildings of Ravello, a popular resort in Campania perching on a natural balcony overlooking the Bay of Salerno. The city still lives up to the name given it centuries ago by Roman seamen who were shipwrecked on its coast and sheltered in the hills that rise above Amalfi. The site was so welcoming that they dubbed it the *res bella*, or beautiful spot. Since then poets and musicians have not ceased to sing its charms. Boccaccio in the *Decameron* devoted a story to Ravello, both lauding its rich merchants and also marvelling at the perils they endured in their trade:

> A merchant from Ravello in Calabria, whose name was Landolfo Ruffolo, failing to sell his goods in Cyprus sold his ship, bought a smaller one and set up as a pirate. Having gained much booty, he in his turn was attacked, looted and captured by the Genovese. The hulk on which they were sailing broke itself on a reef. Clinging to a floating packing case, Landolfo survived. On the coast of the island of Gulfe he was rescued by a woman who was washing her linen. Opening the packing case, Landolfo found a cache of superb jewels. Thus he returned to Ravello far richer than when he left.

By the tenth century Ravello was a wealthy and independent city. Three centuries

LEFT
A superb fountain graces the cloisters of Monreale cathedral, whose pointed arches and delicate patterns display the Arabic influence on Sicilian romanesque architecture.

OVERLEAF LEFT
All the vitality of Norman architecture in Sicily is displayed in this multiple column and capital from the cloister of Monreale cathedral

OVERLEAF RIGHT
The crypt of Villa Cimbrone, Ravello.

later its merchants were still amongst the most prosperous of the Occident. They cultivated the architects who were fostered in Sicily by the Normans; trading with the east, they were receptive to a touch of artistic exoticism; and, as we shall see, they incorporated Saracen elements in the architecture of their majestic buildings.

Centuries later, Wagner cherished this spot as much as Boccaccio had done, and here he composed *Parsifal*. Ravello still beguiles. 'The contrast between its bold situation and its seductive and richly coloured setting, between the rusticity of its hilly streets and the delicate perfection of its works of art, between the gaiety of its gardens and the melancholy of its Norman-Saracenic architecture, is extraordinarily impressive', wrote an Italian tourist in the 1920s. Yet in spite of its fine hotels (some of them, such as the Hotel Caruso Belvedere which stands opposite the twelfth-century church and campanile of San Giovanni del Toro, created from eleventh-century villas), and in spite of its thrustful tourist board, Ravello has thankfully remained a quietly dozy town. 'Here is a keener air,' wrote André Gide in *The Immoralist* (1902), 'the charm of its rocks, with their recesses and their surprises, as well as the unplumbed depths of its valleys, all of which strengthened me and deepened my enjoyment, stimulating my zest for life.'

Because of the mass of tourists, no-one today will experience the same depth of peace enjoyed by André Gide. But I find it nostalgic to re-read his description of this heart-tugging site, if only because it so coincides with my own memories of the place. 'Close by the shore and almost touching the sky, Ravello rises on an abrupt precipice opposite the flat, far coast of Paestum,' he wrote. 'When the Normans dominated the city it was of considerable significance. Today it is merely a narrow village where, I believe, we were the sole strangers. Our lodging was a former religious house now transformed into a hotel. Situated on the vertiginous edge of the cliff, its terraces and gardens seem to be suspended over an azure abyss. A glimpse over the vine-festooned wall offered initially no more than the sea. A closer, sheerer look discovered the steep, cultivated slope down which paths (or rather, staircases) lead from Ravello to the shore.'

He looked up from the centre of the town and saw enormous olive and carob trees, with cyclamens thriving in their shade. Above there were lemon trees and hundreds of Spanish chestnuts. Gide warmed to the lemon groves, threaded by narrow paths. 'One enters them noiselessly,' he wrote, 'like a thief in the night.' The thick, heavy foliage blocked out every ray of sunshine. Perfumed lemons hung green and white in the shade, like 'drops of opaque wax'. Hungry and thirsty Gide plucked them, 'sweet, sharp and refreshing'.

As you enter Ravello you immediately come across a church which combines romanesque with something more exotic. Santa Maria a Gradillo was built in the twelfth century, its architecture – especially the campanile – reflecting in its pointed arches the Arab influence that so much permeates this part of Italy, its nobility in no way fazed by the remains of a thirteenth-century castle built up against it. Scarcely a step away stretches the Piazza Vescovado, dominated by Ravello's cathedral and the complex arches of its thirteenth-century campanile. Although the eleventh-century romanesque *duomo* was considerably rebuilt in the late eighteenth century, no-one was foolish

Atrani sits just below Ravello on the Bay of Salerno.

The mosaic-encrusted pulpit of Ravello cathedral was made by Niccolò di Bartolomeo da Foggia in 1272.

A corner of the eleventh-century Sala d'Aspetto in Villa Rufolo, Ravello.

enough to molest its bronze doors. Barisano da Trani created their fifty-four panels in 1179, leaving for posterity a Byzantine vision of scenes from the Passion of Jesus. Scholars point out that the artist must have copied medieval ivories. He did so with innovative arrogance, and the cathedral authorities at Ravello rightly protect his bronze panels with wooden doors.

Those who designed the interior of Ravello cathedral were careful to live up to the glory of the great bronze doors. The mosaic-encrusted pulpit was created by Niccolò di Bartolomeo da Foggia in 1272, the little lions that support its twisted pillars suggesting toys turned into stone. Some 200, or even 250 years earlier, an unknown artist designed the ambo opposite, from which the gospel would be read, its mosaic depicting Jonah and the whale. These artistic masterpieces are as nothing, the verger told me, compared with the phial of St Pantaleon's blood in the chapel named after the saint, for the dried, ruby-black substance liquifies twice a year, on 19 May and 27 August. Appropriately, St Pantaleon is the patron saint of medical men. According to the tales of Neapolitan grandmothers, he has another miraculous attribute: he can expand to more than twice his normal length. Mothers exasperated by their naughty children still quell their wickedness by threatening that the rubbery saint will stretch up to their bedrooms and carry them away.

In the cathedral square stands Villa Rufolo, built in the thirteenth century, now a museum where a tour of ancient pre-Christian sarcophagi is accompanied by a breathtaking panorama of the bay. As Boccaccio put it, here 'a palace with a beautiful expansive courtyard rises over innumerable evergreen shrubs and plants'. The sole

English pope, Nicholas Brakespeare (who on election adopted the name Adrian IV), took refuge here in the mid twelfth century (and so would I, were I elected pope). Villa Rufolo boasts a convent-style cloister and lush gardens, where in 1880 Richard Wagner was vouchsafed a vision of the enchanted garden of Klingsor, the hero of his *Parsifal*. On 26 May 1880 he wrote in the villa's visitors' book, 'The spellbound garden of Klingsor is discovered.'

In other places it is the conqueror's jackboot which is most in evidence. In 1167 the belligerent Normans took the Sicilian hill fortress of Erice from the Saracens. Believing that this victory had been clinched by the miraculous appearance of St Julian, who drove off the enemy with a pack of hounds, they renamed it Monte San Giuliano. The town became Erice again only in 1934. Long before the Normans it had been settled by the Phoenicians, the Semitic trading nation whose ships travelled the known world and who had dubbed Monte San Giuliano Eryx and made the hill sacred to the goddess Astarte. Later, under the Greeks, Eryx became famous throughout the Mediterranean world for its Temple of Venus Erycina, which Virgil declared was founded by no less a hero than the legendary Trojan Aeneas himself. Although the 270-metre peak on which Erice stands seems impregnable, the hilltown changed hands again and again in the wars between the Sicilian Greeks and the Carthaginians from North Africa.

Three Norman gateways are set in walls constructed of massive blocks dating from the fifth century BC and topped by Norman reinforcements. The Romanesque is already building on the Roman. The inhabitants of Erice, known today for their ceramics and carpets, squeeze themselves into streets blessed with romanesque and gothic doorways, and with little squares and pavements of delicate stones set in remarkably varied patterns.

Here the spirit of the Middle Ages flames unquenched if mildly. On the foundations of a second temple of Venus was built the Chiesa Matrice, which boasts a fine rose window and a campanile of 1312 which predates the church itself by two years. Here, the Madonna has triumphed over the Phoenician goddess Astarte, the Greek goddess Aphrodite and the Roman goddess Venus. But the chief evocation of the Norman past at Erice is to be found in the public garden at the summit of the hill, often bathed in mist. Where the Phoenicians and Greeks worshipped their Gods, the Normans built castles. Behind the first *castello* rises a second one, the so-called Castello di Venere, built in the twelfth and thirteenth centuries. In the walls of this castle the Normans incorporated stones from the former Temple of Venus Erycina, the remains of which, including its holy well, the Pozzo di Venere, are sheltered within the ruins. The view must have been as extraordinary then as it is now, reaching as far as Tunisia on an exceptionally fine day.

In spite of expansion as a tourist resort and a population increase from a mere 3500 in the 1930s to 15,500 today, Erice still seems to me to preserve the essence of romanesque at its most defensive and martial. Spello in Umbria, though properly defending itself as any ancient city needed to, offers a far gentler aspect. An entrancing city of pink-and-white stone, often rough hewn, with long narrow bricks adding a decorative touch, its aura is that of the romanesque in its graceful rather than its mighty aspect. Spello is an

RIGHT
Sicilian-Arabic fantasy: the Cortile Moresco of Villa Rufolo at Ravello.

OVERLEAF
A typically misty view over the mountains from Erice.

elongated triangle, pierced by a Roman thoroughfare. Situated not so much on a hill as on a slope of Monte Subasio, it breathes an air of spaciousness, housing no more than 7600 citizens. Nothing like so ancient as Erice, its name derives from the Roman Hispellum, and the walls are Roman in origin. Much rebuilt, they nevertheless retain their Roman gates, and one of these, the Porta Consolare, arches over the road that climbs up from Foligno. Built during the reign of the Emperor Augustus (63 BC–AD 14), it is decorated with three Roman statues of even earlier date and capped by a powerful medieval tower.

Even though some of its towers support trees, Spello has the comforting feeling of a cared-for place, decked out with roses, vines, sheltered gardens and flowers in pots. The citizens have the pleasing habit of placing Roman remains against the walls of their important buildings. Cypresses set off the houses, and the steep streets offer unexpected vistas of the fertile countryside that surrounds the town. It is easy enough to look inside the courtyards of many of the larger houses, most of them boasting their own wells, others with colonnades and gardens.

The city may seem haphazard, but every element – walls, churches, squares, two-storeyed houses, arches and narrow streets that at times are as steep as staircases – fits together like an intricate puzzle. The main square of Spello, the Piazza Comunale, is reached through the Porta Venere, called after a temple to Venus which once stood close by. Three Roman arches are dwarfed by two huge twelve-sided romanesque towers flanking them and sprouting the usual Umbrian weeds and trees. The street plan surrounding the piazza is redolent of the Middle Ages. Wide steps to the left of the outer courtyard of the thirteenth-century Loggia pass under another arch and descend a narrow flight of steps to reach the delightfully irregular Piazzetta del Municipia, which

The Porta Urbica, one of the five Roman gateways into Spello.

is flanked by pink-and-white houses. From here a narrow street tunnels back up to Via due Ponti and to the front of the church of San Lorenzo. Its once exquisite rose windows are alas clumsily filled in. Built in 1120, partly utilizing stones from a church which had stood here since 560, romanesque San Lorenzo still carries a Roman funeral inscription on its façade. To the north, Via Garibaldi burrows its way up past the little thirteenth-century church of San Martino, its west windows tiny, displaying but two lights. The street winds as far as the Belvedere, where Roman remains have been tamed into a children's playground. As the infants run screaming around you, you can drink in the view of Spello's former amphitheatre and of the twelfth-century romanesque church of San Claudio beyond, a harmonious building with a brick double belfry rising above the stone façade of its regular west end, pierced by a typically delicate Umbrian rose window. Steps rise to the façade of another twelfth-century church, San Severino, today

The main doorway of the cathedral at Todi hovers between romanesque and early gothic.

The great medieval buildings of Todi, seen from the cathedral steps. Ahead is the Palazzo dei Priori, with its tower of 1293. The Palazzo del Popolo of 1233, with swallow-tail crenellations, occupies the far left-hand corner of the square, and beside it is the Palazzo del Capitano of 1290, with its triple gothic windows.

a house of God run by minor Capuchin friars. Here too are the remains of Spello's fourteenth-century *rocca*, with a pink-and-white stone tower sporting brick battlements.

Three more romanesque churches underline Spello's former importance: Santa Barbara near the Piazza Vallegloria; the unpretentious Sant'Andrea (containing a huge painting of the Madonna by Pintoricchio); and the much more glamorous Santa Maria Maggiore. Inside this last is the beautiful Capella Baglioni, a reminder of the unsavoury Baglioni family, who governed Spello in the mid fifteenth century and paid for the chapel. They also employed Pintoricchio to paint its frescoes. The artist was proud enough of this work to include himself amongst the onlookers in the scenes depicting the birth and childhood of Jesus. Not long afterwards, in his extreme old age, Perugino frescoed an enthroned Madonna with her dead son in this church.

Todi, like Spello, is a triangle, this time almost isosceles. Its three points, north, south-west and south-east, rest on three hills dominating the Tiber valley. At the northernmost corner is the Porta Perugina. Set in medieval walls rising from magnificent Roman ramparts which shore up the city, the crumbling white stones of this twelfth-century gateway seem to encapsulate the whole of Todi's history: an Etruscan frontier town taken over by the Romans which in the Middle Ages flourished as a free commune before sinking into oblivion. Todi lost her autonomy in 1368. Somehow her nobility managed to continue building themselves the fine palaces that pop up here and there among her narrow streets.

Todi's cathedral is a romanesque building of the twelfth century, spiced with a hint of gothic. A wide flight of steps rises invitingly up to its simple, pale pink façade. One large and two smaller rose windows surmount the three doorways and a double-storeyed square tower carries the bells. The interior, though unfussy, possesses its due quota of minor masterpieces: a fresco of the Last Judgment, painted by Ferraù da Faenza in the sixteenth century: choir-stalls carved in 1530; a couple of fourteenth-century statues by Andrea Pisano and a couple of paintings by Giovanni di Pietro (1450–1528), Perugino's disciple, who was known as Spagna. The most rewarding work of art is the crucifix of the twelfth or early thirteenth century – a green elongated Christ stretched on a Byzantine cross – while the most satisfying part of the whole cathedral is the twelfth-century crypt, with its mighty apse. Before you leave the upper church, examine the delicately executed late romanesque capitals. I do not know why some historians insist on describing them as gothic.

Immediately south is one of the most entrancing medieval squares in Umbria, the Piazza Vittorio Emanuele II. Its southern flank is guarded by the Palazzo dei Priori, built between 1293 and 1337, its façade crenellated, its windows of 1514 early renaissance. The sculpted eagle decorating this building is the symbol of Todi, since legend has it that the city was founded by a determined man named Tudero who was picnicking on the plain below when such a bird of prey plucked up his tablecloth and deposited it on the top of the hill. Look carefully and you can see the cloth between the eagle's legs. Bounding the piazza to the east are two palaces which today serve as the town hall and the city art gallery and museum. Spagna painted a *Coronation of the Virgin* which hangs here. This picture is a fascinating oddity, for it was commissioned as a copy of one by Ghirlandaio. (Ghirlandaio's prototype now hangs in the gallery at Narni.) Nearly every critic agrees that Spagna has improved on the original; and he has set the Virgin in a gentle Umbrian landscape.

The Palazzo del Popolo dates from 1233 and the Palazzo del Capitano from 1290 (though work continued on it intermittently until 1357). The fourteenth century is frequently said to be the great epoch of Italian town halls. If so, Todi was a pioneer, asserting her civic pride with these two thirteenth-century masterpieces. Massive arcades pierce the Palazzo del Capitano, slightly less formidable ones the Palazzo del Popolo. Both benefit from an elegant flight of steps supported on a mighty half arch. Three gothic windows lighten the Palazzo del Capitano, while battlements with swallow-tail crenellations add a fierce charm to the Palazzo del Popolo.

In the Piazza del Mercato Vecchio, ancient Rome unexpectedly puts in an appearance in the shape of four grandiose Roman arches. These *nicchioni romani*, though pockmarked with age, are still impressive. Once they must have supported a Roman basilica. Today they carry a couple of medieval houses which have seen nobler times, two renaissance arched windows in the façades now reduced by brick infilling. One of them boasts a balcony whose iron balustrade today is fit only for supporting a TV aerial.

Close by (in Via Mercato Vecchio) stands what I regard as one of the humblest and yet most satisfying romanesque churches in Todi. Sant'Ilario (later known as San Carlo) was consecrated in 1249, Its rose window is virtually unadorned. Rising from the west façade is a two-tier romanesque belfry, slender columns dividing each tier into three lights. Inside is a late fifteenth-century painting of the Madonna of Mercy by Spagna.

Further east stands the great gothic church of San Fortunato. Begun in 1292, San Fortunato crowns a wide flight of steps, flanked by trim hedges and neat green lawns which serve to point up the white stone of its unfinished west façade, added in the first half of the fifteenth century. Only the main entrance sets out to achieve any kind of monumentality, and even here the delicacy of the treatment remains harmonious with the rest of the church. The architect of this doorway was Giovanni di Santuccio da Fiorenzuola of Spoleto, helped by his nephew Bartolo d'Angelo. The campanile, topped with a pyramid, dates from 1460.

Statues of the Virgin and the Angel Gabriel flank the portal. Inside are several treats, including inlaid choir-stalls of 1590 by Antonio Maffei of Gubbio and – in the fourth chapel on the right – a remarkable painting of the Madonna and Child with two angels. Executed by Masolino da Panicale in 1432, it is remarkable because of its subtle perspective. Masolino was a friend and collaborator of Masaccio, and together they experimented with new rules of perspective that were to revolutionize fifteenth-century art. Although Masaccio (1401–28) has been given most credit for this new direction in painting, no-one should underestimate the contribution of Masolino, as this apparently simple masterpiece demonstrates. San Fortunato itself represents a turning point in Italian church architecture. As at San Domenico in Perugia (which was begun in 1305), the architects of San Fortunato decided to make the aisles the same height as the nave, thus increasing the spaciousness of the building and producing one of the earliest Italian examples of a hall-church. Conscious of his daring, the architect took the precaution of supporting the arches of the aisles with extra cross-pieces three-quarters of the way up.

The crypt shelters the tomb of Christ's troubadour, the poet and mystic Brother Jacopone da Todi, who died in 1307. Author of the first Italian Christmas carol, Jacopone fell foul of Pope Benedict VIII, who disliked the Franciscan's excessive passion for poverty and excommunicated him. Pope Benedict XI showed greater sense and in 1304 lifted the excommunication. His predecessor had condemned a man whose sublime *Stabat Mater* has been sung in Holy Week by countless Christians who have never heard of Benedict VIII:

The sinuous, complex columns of the porch of San Fortunato, Todi.

Jesus, may thy cross defend me,
And thy saving death befriend me,
　　Cherished by thy deathless grace;
When to dust my dust returneth,
Grant a soul that to thee yearneth,
　　In thy Paradise a place.

After the completion of San Fortunato, Todi slept, politically and architecturally, and in 1523 a plague took off over half of the population. The church of San Prassede, with its pink-and-white façade, has still not been completed. Then Angelo Cesi became bishop and initiated a final architectural spurt, one that served to point up the essential romanesque ambience of the place by bringing in a totally different style. The new bishop built himself an episcopal palace (the Palazzo Cesi) by the cathedral steps. To the south-west, outside the city walls, was an unfinished church, Santa Maria della Consolazione. Bishop Cesi decided that it must be completed. In 1508 the first architect, Colo da Caprarola, under the influence of Bramante, had planned a church in the shape of a Greek cross, a revolutionary enough renaissance building with two polygonal apses and a third semicircular apse to the north. Ambroglio Barocci da Milano took over, and the dome was finally added in 1607. Ippolito Scalza contributed twelve vigorous statues of angels to the church.

This is the entrancing white building that greets those who climb up to the Porta Orvetano. It appears again amidst trees and green fields as you look down from the park that has been made out of Todi's ruined fourteenth-century *rocca*. But Bishop Cesi was not content with one renaissance church outside the walls of his romanesque city. A kilometre east of Todi by way of the Porta Romana rises another church designed as a Greek cross. The Tempio del Crocifisso was begun in 1593 by Valentino Martelli, continued two years later by Ippolito Scalza, and finally domed in 1740. With this building Todi decided to stay its architectural hand.

Osimo in the rich tablelands of the Marches not far from Ancona also seems suspended in time. Known as Auximium to the Romans, who colonized Osimo in 157 BC, the city dominated the valleys of the Musone and the Aspio and guards within its walls renaissance and baroque buildings as well as romanesque delights. These last, however, are what linger in the mind. The cathedral itself derives from that moment in architectural history when the romanesque was being tantalised by an incipient gothic. Do not miss the magnificent bronze font in its baptistery, created by Pietro Paolo Iacometti in 1627, or the fourth-century sarcophagus in the crypt. The city's thirteenth-century Palazzo del Comune, which has happily preserved its romanesque campanile, is the home today of a remarkable collection of Roman sculptures, including a celebrated head of an old man chiselled in the first century BC. Alas, when the Milanese captured Osimo in the sixteenth century, they were vandals enough to mutilate most of these priceless pieces.

If Osimo, Todi and Spello illustrate the unexpected variety of Italy's romanesque hilltowns, Massa Marittima in Tuscany is more complex than any of them. The city is

The church of San Filippo Neri lends it classical stateliness to Osimo.

divided into two parts, the lower, walled *città vecchia* and the upper *città nuova*. The *città vecchia* is the honey-pot for lovers of the romanesque. Between 1228 and 1304 Pisan architects built there a cathedral in the style already made famous in their own city. It rises from a majestic flight of steps in the Piazza Garibaldi, the seven blind arches of the lower façade carrying a loggia of ten more arches. Carved men and women, lions, horses and griffins scamper here, the whole façade enlivened by the colourful white, green and red marble out of which it is created.

The portal carries a sculptured biography of St Cerbone, patron saint of the city, who died around 380. His life was scarcely peaceful, though he died in his sleep and not a martyr. Born in Africa, he was driven thence by the Vandals and escaped to Tuscany with his crony St Regulus. Cerbone became Bishop of Populonia, where the heathen sentenced him to be killed by wild animals. Fortunately, several sympathetic Roman soldiers hid him and he escaped to Elba, where he spent the last thirty years of his earthly life. Today he lies in the crypt of the cathedral in a magical marble tomb, sculpted by Goro di Gregorio in 1324 with eight scenes from his life. St Cerbone, along with the Blessed Virgin Mary, is also patron of the cathedral, and the frescoed west end of the church is pierced by a fourteenth-century stained-glass window depicting him visiting Pope Vigilius. Other works of art worth searching out in the cathedral include the font and its cover in the first chapel on the right. Giroldo da Como created the font in 1267, covering it with biblical scenes, including one of the beheading of St John the Baptist. Fired by this grim scene, the sculptor of the elaborate mid fifteenth-century cover decorated it with representations of the Twelve Apostles and, crowning them all, John the Baptist. Finally, look for Duccio di Buoninsegna's portrait of the Madonna, dated 1316, which hangs in a chapel to the left of the high altar, and for the late thirteenth-century crucifix which Segna di Bonaventura painted for a chapel in the right transept.

Opposite the cathedral in the slightly sloping piazza stands the Palazzo Comunale. In truth it comprises three buildings, a tower dating from the thirteenth century (on which Urbano da Cortona in 1468 carved the she-wolf of Siena, Massa Marittima's ally), a façade of the fourteenth century by the Sienese architects Stefano di Méo and Gualtiero di Sozzo, and an interior constructed 200 years later. Even more beautiful is the romanesque Palazzo Pretorio, built in the first half of the thirteenth century and decorated with thirty coats of arms of the leaders of the city from 1426 to 1633. Today this *palazzo* serves as the archaeological museum and art gallery (the latter housing a justly famous early fourteenth-century *Maestà* by Ambrogio Lorenzetti). In the upper city rises the early thirteenth-century Torre Candeliere, a tower linked by a long archway to the ramparts of the ruined fourteenth-century fortress which the Sienese built after they had conquered Massa Marittima in 1353. Surprisingly, the *rocca* shelters a gothic church, Sant'Agostino, built mostly between 1299 and 1313, though the apse was not finished until 1348.

As Massa Marittima shows, any tour of Italy's romanesque hilltowns soon reveals strong regional differences in architectural style. The Pisans loved polychrome décors, and superimposing arcades and colonnades one atop the other. Umbrian architects, on

69

the other hand, achieved their most stunning effects with quiet and orderly sculpture. The best way of comparing domestic Pisan romanesque with the Umbrian variety is to visit the isolated hill capped by Lugnano in Teverina with Massa Marittima still in one's memory. Inside the medieval walls of Lugnano in Teverina, the twelfth-century church of Santa Maria Assunta in Piazza Umberto I, like the cathedral at Massa Marittima, is replete with carved animals and human beings; but here the symbols of the evangelists over the porch are well-behaved, conscious of the vast weight of Christian lore they bear. Inside, everything is severe as well as graceful. Eight massive round pillars support the roof, their capitals sometimes decorated with scampering human beings. The pavement is a cool mosaic. The pulpit is chastely decorated. A romanesque baldacchino shelters the high altar. Another eight romanesque pillars, as slender as those of the nave are massy, support the crypt. Nicolò Alunno's triptych in the apse,

Romanesque Umbria: Santa Maria Assunta, Lugnano in Teverina.

*The Ascending Virgin supported by Saints Francis and Sebastian*, seems almost too exuberant for this austere church.

The *città vecchia* of Lugnano in Teverina is quintessentially romanesque, its church of Santa Maria Assunta the most perfect romanesque religious house in Umbria. What these hilltowns and cities reveal above all is that romanesque architecture is a supple and remarkably varied art-form. Monterrigioni in Tuscany, for instance, a superb medieval hilltown whose fourteen defensive towers reminded Dante of the frightful giants who guard the ninth circle of hell and whose long main street bisects the town from one gate to another, has a parish church which has retained a simple romanesque façade. The lines of this façade are far less sophisticated than those of the twelfth-century romanesque church built for the Cistercian abbey which stands in the village of Abbadio Isola a mere three kilometres east. Equally unpretentious is Montegabbione,

The quintessentially romanesque interior of Santa Maria Assunta.

a fortified romanesque village set 594 metres above sea-level north of Orvieto. Its buttressed watchtower is a tenth-century romanesque construction. The parish church hints at the gothic, but its basic structure, with a little round west window, remains romanesque, as does the infinitely simpler thirteenth-century church of the Madonna delle Grazie.

To move from these villages into a major city that remains essentially, even superlatively romanesque – in spite of some outstanding Roman remains – we must travel to Spoleto. Spoleto boasts a tiny bridge which the Romans built across a river (which was later diverted) in the first century BC. Even the medieval city walls are built on pre-Christian foundations, the traces of which can still be made out. The cathedral rises over the site of a church built by the Romans, while the Piazza del Mercato exactly traces the outlines of the former Roman forum. As for the *rocca*, it is based on the

foundations of a Roman acropolis. Spoleto also ought to offer its visitors the sight of two Roman amphitheatres, but one of them is bizarrely incorporated in the army barracks.

On this Roman base grew up an exquisite medieval city, whose intricate charm owes much to its steeply-sloping hillside site. Sinuous medieval streets wind ever upwards, with all the steep turns and dangerous corners that add exhilaration to driving in an Italian hill city. By the massive *rocca* at the top you can look down over steep cliffs onto an astonishingly tall yet crazily slender structure, the 200-metre long and vertiginously high bridge which the architect Matteo Gattapone built across the ravine in the second half of the fourteenth century. You can even walk over the valley along the narrow parapet of the bridge.

Over to the left from the road down into the city you can see the romanesque church of San Pietro, which lies outside Spoleto's walls, and high on the hill a monastery. The martial *rocca* too has a religious origin. Gattapone built it in 1359 for his patron the papal-legate Cardinal Albornoz. Albornoz was busy reasserting papal authority throughout this part of Italy at the same time as he was reorganizing the papal states. The towers guarding each corner of his castle at Spoleto, not to speak of two more glaring down from the centre of the long walls, are there to demonstrate his deadly seriousness to anyone that might care to stand in his way. Eventually the Rocca Albornoz became a prison, and the fascists used it during World War II to incarcerate their political prisoners. As a notice on the wall satisfyingly records, in October and November 1943 ninety-four Italians and Slovenians escaped from the *rocca* into the nearby mountains. Far from taking time to recuperate from their incarceration, they became the advance guard of the local partisans in the fight against fascism.

A little flight of steps at the furthermost corner of the piazza below the *rocca*, which is enlivened with a seventeenth-century fountain, runs through an archway down into Via Aurelia Saffi, on the right of which is the Piazza del Duomo. A wide flight of steps known as Via dell'Arringo descends to the piazza, across which the fourteenth-century west portico of the cathedral appears like a stage-set, especially when it is floodlit in the evening. Ambroglio Barocci of Milan and Pippo di Antonio of Florence built it some 200 years after the rest of the cathedral was finished. It shelters an understated twelfth-century romanesque façade.

In 1155 the soldiers of the Holy Roman Emperor Frederick Barbarossa had razed an earlier building. In penance the emperor gave the cathedral an icon which it still possesses. The Spoletans responded by creating a new cathedral with no fewer than seven rose windows piercing its façade. They rise in rows, with four rose windows at the lowest level. Above a cornice, columns and caryatids frame a perfectly entrancing central rose. The symbols of Matthew, Mark, Luke and John decorate each corner. At the very end of the twelfth century the cathedral was heightened with another tier. The city outreached itself. Money and enthusiasm ran out, and the final tier was never finished. Two out of three extremely shallow pointed arches, intended for decoration with mosaics, still await embellishment. Only the central one has been finished. It depicts Christ blessing the world. He sits between his mother and St John, the disciple whom Jesus loved. The artist signed the mosaic with his name, Solsterno, adding the

The twelfth-century façade of Spoleto cathedral rises over a renaissance loggia.

OVERLEAF
A glimpse of the church of San Pietro, Spoleto, seen through the arches of Gattapone's bridge.

date – 1207. As for the romanesque campanile, it stands aloof, even more austere than the romanesque façade.

Since Luigi Arrigucci rebuilt the interior of the cathedral in the mid seventeenth century in a florid Florentine style, those who go inside inevitably feel an initial sense of disappointment. (Pope Urban III paid for the reconstruction, and his reward is the bust sculpted by Bernini which you can see on the west wall.) But Spoleto cathedral bristles with works of art. On the right wall of the south transept is a *Madonna, Child and Saints* by Annibale Carracci, while the Chapel of Constantino Eroli was frescoed by Pintoricchio. Most touching, though not necessarily the finest art in the cathedral, is the last work of the Florentine Filippo Lippi, the decoration of the apse. Lippi, by all accounts, was a far from chaste monk who had spent much of his monastic life leaping the wall in search of women. With this superb cycle, which depicts the Angel Gabriel

75

visiting the Virgin Mary, the birth of Jesus, the death of the Virgin and her heavenly Coronation, Filippo Lippi surely redeemed himself. He also painted his own portrait, as well as those of his son and his two assistants (Brother Diamante and Pier Matteo of Amelia). They stand among the crowd in the scene of the death of the Virgin. Filippo Lippi began work on these masterpieces in 1467. Two years later he was dead, his mortal remains sheltered in a tomb designed by his son Filippino which stands in the left transept of the cathedral.

The cathedral square boasts two other fine buildings, the sixteenth-century Palazzo Arroni with its imposing doorway and gracious loggia, and the nineteenth-century Caio Melisso theatre. The latter was designed by Giovanni Mantiroli in 1880 to incorporate an earlier, late seventeenth-century theatre which was judged too small for the needs of his age. Note too the fountain, constructed out of a Roman sarcophagus. Further on

The tranquillity of the early twelfth century: the interior of Sant'Eufemia, Spoleto.

towards the centre of Spoleto rises the fifteenth-century Archbishops' Palace. Today it serves as the diocesan museum of religious art, housing works dating from the thirteenth century onwards. Another romanesque treasure, the early twelfth-century church of Sant'Eufemia, stands in the courtyard of the palace, its delicately unpretentious façade adorned with pale pink bricks. St Eufemia was a virgin martyr, victim of the persecutions of the Emperor Diocletian (245–313). She miraculously survived countless tortures until her persecutors tossed her to the mercy of wild beasts. No aura of her tormented life permeates her church, whose interior, unchanged for eight centuries, is unusually complex in design and remarkably calm in atmosphere. Frequently it houses a Christian appeal to help the afflicted of our own times. This is the sole Umbrian church to have been built with a gallery reserved for women.

The church of Santissimi Giovanni e Paolo, consecrated in 1174, affords an

The fearsome mid seventeenth-century Mascherone fountain, set in a wall beside the romanesque church of Santi Simone e Giuda, Spoleto.

opportunity of comparing a much richer romanesque church with the complex calm of Sant'Eufemia. This church has now been deconsecrated and you can visit it only in the morning. If you can find your way there in time to look inside, you will be rewarded with two particularly interesting frescoes: one of them is among the earliest portraits of St Francis of Assisi and therefore free of the mythological accretions which soon attached themselves to the image of this saint; the other depicts the martyrdom of the English saint Thomas Becket, another example of the remarkable way in which the cult of this martyr spread so rapidly across Europe.

Another forgotten church, San Nicolò di Bari, lies in the spacious Piazza Edmondo de Amicis, with a gracious arched doorway giving onto the square. The adjoining cloister, now splendidly restored, is well worth a visit. (Restoration was certainly necessary: the church had been deconsecrated in the last century and transformed first into an ironworks and then into a covered market selling truffles and cloth.) This monastery, founded in 1304, was once the centre of renaissance humanism in Spoleto. A plaque tells you that the great Reformer Martin Luther stayed here in 1512, though at this time he had not yet turned against the papacy. In fact, it was in that year that he was made both a Doctor of Divinity and sub-prior of his own convent at Wittenberg.

Via Gregorio Elladio leads north from the church past the cloister wall, eventually reaching a thirteenth-century tower. Nearby, still set in medieval walls, is the powerful twelfth-century Porta Fuga, 'gate of flight'. As a Latin inscription informs us, it is also called Hannibal's gate, not because Hannibal took the town but because, having routed the troops of the Roman general Flaminius near Lake Trasimeno in 217 BC, he arrived here to find the Spoletans more than his equal. Hannibal promptly fled.

Steps climb back to Via Gregorio Elladio. Close by, rising pink and white, stands another church whose history stems from the romanesque era. Vast San Domenico was begun in the thirteenth century and finished in the fifteenth. Amongst the touching frescoes of its single vast nave, I like best a heart-rending *Deposition* on the left-hand wall. Over the high altar hangs a crucifixion painted on wood in the fourteenth century. Blood spurts viciously from Jesus's side. Within a moment visitors can reach a *palazzo* utterly remote from this medieval spirituality, the Palazzo Collicola, which Sebastiano Cipriani built in 1737, using every device to give an impression of luxury. Then the romanesque appears again, up the steps opposite this *palazzo* and along Via Plinio il Giovane, where stands the deconsecrated church of San Lorenzo. Twelfth-century, carrying a belfry with two little bells, the church is decorated inside with delicate thirteenth- and fourteenth-century frescoes.

The streets of Spoleto continue to climb and twist from here to the thirteenth- and fourteenth-century fortified Palazzo Corvi. Next to this palace is yet another deconsecrated romanesque church, Sant'Agata. Two stone pillars with simple carved foliage for capitals hold up its arcade. Even higher up is the Piazza della Libertà. Suddenly romanesque Spoleto becomes Roman Spoleto. Steps at the corner of the seventeenth-century Palazzo Ancaiani lead down into the excavated arcades and stepped seats of one of the Roman amphitheatres, the stage now occupied by the apse of the church of Sant'Agata.

As a plaque declares, the corner house of Via Brignone across the piazza was once the home of Francesco Possenti. The eleventh child of thirteen, he was born in 1838 and educated by the local Jesuits. For a while he lived the life of a fop. In the words of the hagiographer Fr Bernard Kelly, 'Drawing room parties, theatricals, society gossip, and above all dancing, were now as serious objects in life to Francis as the classical and philosophy course at the Jesuit College.' The biographer continues, 'He dressed not merely in the latest mode, but sometimes even, as people say, a little beyond it – used habitually a quantity of scent and parted his hair "with meticulous care!"' Illness and bereavement, Fr Bernard judged, 'began to bring Francis Possenti to his senses'. Soon the budding saint had contracted consumption. If God cured him, he vowed, he too would become a Jesuit. Apparently cured, he took the name Gabriele dell'Addolorata (Gabriel of Our Lady of Sorrows), becoming not a Jesuit but a member of the Passionist order. Never resting in his desire to discover better and better ways of mortifying his body, he wore himself out. Moreover, his previous sickness had not been cured, and Francesco Possenti died of tuberculosis aged only twenty-four. In 1920 he was canonized under the name of St Gabriel of Our Lady of Sorrows.

Although Via Brignone is flanked by the seventeenth-century Palazzo Mauri, this is still essentially Roman Spoleto. Ahead rises the third-century BC Roman gate known today as the Arco di Monterone. To the left along Via dell'Arco di Druso is an even finer Roman arch, built over two centuries after the Arco di Monterone by the senate of Spoleto in honour of the son of the Emperor Tiberius. Next door, the eighteenth century church of Sant'Isacco has a twelfth-century crypt and a charming cloister,

abutting onto a former Roman temple. And not far away is the Casa Romana, a gloomy Roman house built in the first century AD.

Still more of Spoleto remains romanesque, in particular the churches of San Salvatore (with its frescoed crypt) and of San Gregorio Maggiore (built in its present form between 1179 and 1246 and again boasting a fine crypt). The portico of San Gregorio dates from the sixteenth century, its powerful campanile from the eleventh. Though fine, none of them is as splendid as San Pietro, just outside the city by way of the third-century Monterone gate. The twelfth-century façade is carved with men fighting lions, Jesus walking on the water and human legs dangling helplessly from a devil's cooking-pot. A peasant works in his fields with oxen and his dog. A doe fends off a serpent. The Archangel Gabriel is here, weighing souls, finding them wanting in the balance and abandoning them to the devil. The seventeenth-century interior is richly decorated with crimson damask embroidered with gold braid. Above the high altar hangs a golden baldacchino.

The road from this church snakes up to Monteluco, offering superb views of Spoleto as it curves. On a corner to the right rises another romanesque church, the twelfth-century San Giuliano, its porch incorporating fragments of the sixth-century house of God which it replaced. Monteluco itself stands 830 metres above sea-level. Panoramas appear to right and left. Here St Francis founded a convent, and the sanctuary is still open to visitors. Underneath the trees emerge hotels and a bar.

The subsequent history of all these medieval towns decided whether they remained romanesque or their architecture developed. Some prospered, attracted rich immigrants and new monastic orders, and were rebuilt; others simply dozed. The spiritual needs of Trevi, rising on a hill which overlooks the Spoletan plain, were for long served simply by one church, the exquisite Sant'Emiliano, which was built in the twelfth century. Only in 1213, when St Francis himself brought his friars here, did the Christians of Trevi build the thirteenth-century early gothic church which bears his name. Just as the aura of one of Italy's saintliest figures can here momentarily blind us to the romanesque riches of Trevi, so I often think that at Certaldo, half-way between Siena and Florence, the memory of one of Italy's most subtly salacious authors, Giovanni Boccaccio, makes one neglect the town's equally splendid romanesque remains. Although Boccaccio was born in Paris, he spent most of his life at Certaldo, where he died in 1375. His home, which was restored in the nineteenth century and then again after the air raids of World War II, is a fascinating national museum dedicated to the study above all of his *Decameron*. The writer lies buried in the thirteenth-century church of Santissimi Michele e Jacopo, though in 1783 his funeral monument was destroyed by puritans outraged by his writings. Certaldo also boasts the fifteenth-century Palazzo Pretorio, frescoed in part by Benozzo Gozzoli. Yet in spite of these treasures, what I find most delightful in this town is the gentle romanesque façade of the church of San Tommaso in Via Rivellino, the pleasure of seeing it enhanced by the neighbouring romanesque cloister of 1210, especially when they are illuminated by a shaft of sunlight and look so fragile that a sudden puff of wind might at any moment blow them both away.

A distant view of Trevi.

# 3

# THE FLOWERING OF
# THE MIDDLE AGES

BY THE END of the thirteenth century Europe was more prosperous than ever before, and the most affluent country of all was Italy. Italian merchants were at the centre of a remarkable international empire of commerce. From the Orient they brought medicines and textiles, dyes and spices, silks and slaves, to be sold in Europe or exchanged for Flemish cloth and English wool. This imported cloth and wool was then transformed into luxurious textiles by skilled Italian craftsmen, and the results of their work were then re-exported. By the fourteenth century, although the sheep bred in Italy were of poorer quality than those of England or northern France, this trade had become so profitable that the Italians were also producing their own cloth. And the wheels of this commercial empire were oiled by the richest banking houses in the world.

Yet the country was remarkably fragmented. The dominant forces in society were the towns, over which no-one managed to exert any central authority. The Holy Roman Emperor, nominally ruler of Italy, was obliged to spend much of his time in other parts of his empire. When the papacy attempted to impose its authority through local bishops, the oligarchies who ruled the towns resolutely resisted the attempts of these outsiders to take control over their affairs. At the same time, these rulers were often at odds with each other and leading families increasingly built fortresses for themselves within a town to assert their own power. Only when their differences seemed irreconcilable were they forced to bring in an outsider (known as the *podestà*), whose task was not simply to rule but to attempt also to act as a mediator.

In the thirteenth century the rule of the aristocracy was challenged by a new, moneyed class, the *popolo grasso*, an upper bourgeoisie consisting of prosperous merchants, the professional classes, skilled craftsmen and newly risen bankers. To assert its own power, not just in the face of the rulers of the towns but also over the artisans and lower orders, members of the *popolo grasso* began organizing themselves into guilds. In greater cities, such as Perugia or Siena, the structure of the guilds was elaborate, often with elected masters and councillors. Inevitably such groups claimed a share of civic power.

These rich laymen and women were increasingly well educated. Some men doubted whether women ought to be taught to read. Paolo da Certaldo, for example, in his *Libro di Buoni Costumi* written in *c.*1350, suggested that although boys ought to begin reading at six or seven, women, save for nuns, should be taught only to sew. Others

The sun-drenched Tuscan landscape between Certaldo and San Gimignano.

proposed singing and dancing as more suitable occupations. Although the suggested alternatives reveal the sweetening of life made possible by money, the thirst for books was unquenchable amongst the educated. Lives of the saints (especially of St Francis), vernacular poetry (such as that written by Jacopone da Todi or Folgòre da San Gimignano), the historical annals produced in monasteries, and tales of pilgrimages all proliferated. Boccaccio's *Decameron* appeared just as Paolo da Certaldo was fretting about the possible evil effects of secular literature on the morals of women. More vigorous pursuits than reading or sewing included jousts, horse-racing and bustling fairs, entertainments which also helped to bolster a communal spirit.

The independence of the Italian towns promoted a powerful civic pride, and much of the wealth that fuelled the ambitions of the citizens went into enhancing their surroundings. Among those who most profited from wealthy patrons were the guilds

formed by artists. Thus, in 1307 the citizens of San Gimignano felt that they lacked a sufficient number of goldsmiths and decided to pay one of their number to train some. And yet, despite this concern with the material things of life and widespread hostility to ecclesiastical pretensions, Italy at this time was paradoxically extremely devout. Religion played the central role in most people's lives. The religious orders flourished and built lavishly, while religious fervour persuaded many laypeople to set themselves up in confraternities devoted to good works. Of these good works, building great churches or rebuilding older ones in what was considered a more glorious fashion was perceived as of paramount importance.

Around the mid twelfth century, a suppler, more fluid style of architecture appeared in Europe, characterized by pointed vaults and arches. Four centuries later it came to be known as 'gothic', a word used by the men and women of the Renaissance who wished to distinguish their own return to classical forms from the designs and achievements of their predecessors.

France was the birthplace of this gothic style, in particular the church of Saint-Denis near Paris under the rule of the Abbé Suger (who died in 1151). Sens cathedral was the first major building to be constructed entirely in gothic. Lacking any form of transept, its style was infinitely simpler than that of the later gothic masterpieces of European architecture. Soon, especially in north-east France, gothic windows were being designed in increasingly elongated form, their tracery shimmering with sinuous movement. A passageway or triforium set half-way up the soaring walls added to the complexity of the buildings. Stained glass filled the windows of the transepts as well as the nave and apse. Animated statues and capitals copied directly from nature gave a new rhythm to churches, cathedrals and palaces. In the mid thirteenth century the Capetian royal family in France poured its wealth into creating more and more glamorous gothic buildings, and their achievements were transplanted to Italy primarily through the skills of Giovanni Pisano, the son of Nicola. At Siena and at Pisa this genius brought a dramatic intensity to the patterns which he and his father both admired and copied from the models of antiquity.

Dawn on a ridge near Siena.

Germany, Majorca, Greece and Spain also succumbed to this new style, with castles and palaces as well as churches exhibiting the fecundity and exuberance of the gothic spirit. At the same time, the dynastic ambitions of great families brought the styles of their own countries to parts of Italy. Both the German house of Hohenstaufen, several members of which became Holy Roman Emperors, and the Spanish house of Aragon, which ruled Sicily, Sardinia and Naples in the fourteenth and fifteenth centuries, introduced their own artistic and architectural tastes into the peninsula. To some Italian towns these influences and styles came late; but they took such a hold on people's imaginations that they often persisted longer here than anywhere else in Europe.

The genius of this flowering of the Middle Ages is perhaps best seen in the Tuscan hilltown of Siena. From the beginning of the thirteenth century Siena had grown rich on the cloth trade and through money-lending, her merchants establishing bases as far away as northern France and England. By the fourteenth century the city was at the height of its economic prosperity, partly because it lay on the Via Francigena, a major trade route linking France and Rome which also promoted cultural ties and influences. Between 1297 and 1310, funded by this prosperity and inspired by these influences, gothic masters constructed the battlemented Palazzo Pubblico. With its tall slender tower reaching to a height of 102 metres, this palace surpassed virtually every other civic building of its age in artistic ambition and glamour. Some forty years later, as a thanks-offering for the city's relief from the devastating plague of 1348, an exquisitely decorated chapel was added to the palace, making it a superb blend of religious and secular gothic in the Italian style.

Only in the first half of the fourteenth century can one discern a recognizably gothic style of painting in Italy. Again Siena is where it first appears, in the works of two brothers, Pietro and Ambrogio Lorenzetti. Ambrogio was responsible for the frescoes on the theme of *Good and Evil Government* in the Palazzo Pubblico, painted between 1337 and 1339. This revealing masterpiece illuminates more than any other the remarkable political developments of thirteenth- and fourteenth-century Tuscany in which Siena played a central part and without which the Middle Ages could never have flowered as they did.

From 1271 to 1280 the city had been ruled by a group of captains who remained loyal to the papacy in its struggles with the Holy Roman Emperors. After 1280 their hegemony was replaced by that of fifteen men known as governors and defensors. Seven years later these gave way to nine priors, and it is in the room where they deliberated, the *Sala dei Nove*, that Lorenzetti's frescoes are to be found. At the heart of the fresco depicting 'good government' is a single, black-clad figure, surrounded by symbolic representations of justice, concord and peace, as well as the biblical virtues of faith, hope and charity. Justice is here depicted as supremely important, and an inscription proclaims that 'Wherever this sacred virtue reigns, many souls are united, and once united they constitute the Common Good which rules over them.' Lorenzetti also depicted here what he held to be the most beneficent effect of 'good government': prosperity. 'Let all free men go their way without fear,' declares a scroll carried by a naked figure who symbolizes security, 'and let everyone work and sow without fear.' The fresco depicts a prosperous city whose citizens are trading, hunting, making music, practising medicine, working metal, dancing and growing crops. As well as Lorenzetti's *Good and Evil Government*, the *palazzo* also has splendid coffered ceilings and frescoes by such Sienese masters as Simone Martini and Lorenzo di Pietro (who was known as Il Vecchietta and was born here in 1412). Among the masterpieces by Martini is a celebrated *Maestà*, a representation of the Virgin Mary enthroned in heaven, which he painted in 1315. The palace chapel, frescoed with scenes from the life of the Blessed Virgin Mary, is enhanced by a lovely wrought-iron screen.

The Palazzo Pubblico overlooks the unique, shell-shaped Piazza del Campo, where each year horsemen from ten of the city's seventeen districts career around in the most celebrated race in Italy, the Palio. Before the contest, the competing horses are blessed in their parish churches. For the Sienese, this piazza was an expression of their own civic pride. To ensure that no other building in the piazza clashed in style with the Palazzo

Pubblico, in 1297 the city priors decreed that 'if any house or palace around the Palazzo del Mercato shall be rebuilt, each and every one of those windows of the said house or palazzo which overlooks the campo shall have small columns and shall not be made with any form of balcony.' The *podestà* was charged with enforcing this decree (which was re-issued in 1310) and given power to fine those who failed to conform.

In 1347 the piazza was divided into nine segments, symbolizing the nine medieval governors of the city. Again Siena's civic consciousness was being expressed in its town planning. The city itself contributed two-thirds of the cost of the work, while the owners of the properties overlooking the square were asked to pay only one-third. The fountain gushing in the piazza was dubbed 'the joyful one' (*la Gaia*) when it was finished in 1419 by Siena's greatest sculptor, Jacopo della Quercia, an expression of the citizens' welcome to the water itself. In truth this water had been brought to the Campo as early as 1343, five years before the plague carried off two-thirds of the city's population. 'I, Agnolo di Tura, known as "the fat one", buried my five children with my own hands,' wrote one Sienese. 'Throughout the city there were those so poorly covered with earth that the dogs dug them up and gnawed their bodies. No one mourned any death, for everyone expected to die. So many died that everyone believed it to be the end of the world.' The joyful fountain is thus also a symbol of Siena's recovery from that disaster.

According to the sixteenth-century art historian Giorgio Vasari, Jacopo was paid 2200 gold ecus for his fountain, on which representations of the seven virtues and scenes from the Bible surround a carving of the Blessed Virgin Mary. Vasari adds that from that moment to the end of his life the Sienese no longer called him Jacopo della Quercia, but Jacopo della Fonte. His fountain is the sole renaissance masterpiece in sight.

At the north-eastern side of the Campo rises the Palazzo Sansedoni, built in 1339. Narrow streets wind from here between thirteenth-century palaces to the symbol of the city's religious pride, the cathedral. Half romanesque and begun in the twelfth century, its façade was transformed into a riot of polychrome gothic by Giovanni Pisano and his richly talented studio. As for the interior, its walls and columns are decorated with bands of black and white marble and its pavement, 1300 square metres in area, is a masterpiece of marble marquetry. Created over 200 years, from the mid fourteenth till the mid sixteenth century, it includes 56 separate monochrome patterns. A cornice around the nave bears the portrait busts of 172 popes, underneath which the sculpted heads of thirty-six emperors peer from medallions. Among the cathedral's other treasures is a splendid *Assumption*, painted by Il Vecchietta in 1462. This multi-talented renaissance master also gave the cathedral its bronze tabernacle, and Jacopo della Quercia contributed the splendid font. But all these splendours are, I think, eclipsed by the elaborate pulpit which the Pisan Nicola Pisano sculpted in the 1260s. I would judge that the superb *Maestà*, carried in triumph from the workshop of Duccio di Buoninsegna to the high altar in 1311, is its equal, but today you must see his masterpiece in the cathedral museum.

This city bursts with fine churches, among which the brick San Domenico, begun in 1225, should certainly be visited, if only because it houses the relics of the extraordinary

St Catherine of Siena. Constant scourge of the enemies of the papacy, scourge too of those popes whose conduct seemed to her unfitting, Catherine hated the mid fourteenth-century schism of the church which saw Pope Urban VI in Rome suffering a rival anti-Pope Clement VII in Avignon. Longing for martyrdom she died, alas, from natural causes in 1380, aged only thirty-three. For the most part buried in Rome, her skull and a finger were brought back to her native Siena, to comfort the faithful flocking to pray before them in San Domenico. Catherine was but one of Siena's great preachers in its medieval heyday; another was the missionary preacher St Bernardino (who came here to reform the city's Franciscans); and this tradition of eloquence lived into the fifteenth century in the humanism of a future pope, Aeneas Silvius Piccolomini. The gothic of Siena's three finest churches (the cathedral apart), namely San Bernardino, San Francesco and Santa Maria dei Servi, owes its peculiar severity to the influence of the Cistercians, who established a new austerity in architecture throughout Europe.

If Siena is a triumph of medieval town planning, Perugia is a magical warren which still pulsates with medieval exuberance. As Henry James observed of this city, 'On archways and street-staircases and dark alleys that bore through a density of massive basements, and curve and climb and plunge as they go, all to the truest medieval tune, you may feast your fill.' His words sum up the entrancement of the medieval hilltowns and cities of Italy. Lying at the heart of the country, almost equidistant from the Adriatic and the Mediterranean and on the ancient route from Rome to northern Italy, the city of Perugia has been settled and fought over since ancient times – by Etruscans, Romans, settlers from Byzantium, the sixth-century German conquerors of Italy who took the name Lombards, and by the feudal servants of the papacy. Only in my own lifetime has the city burst out from its medieval heart surrounded by Etruscan ramparts. When I first visited Perugia in the mid 1950s she still preserved her ancient aspect inviolate. Sadly, the gentle slopes running down to the Tiber below the walls were disfigured by speculators in the 1960s.

To perceive history through stone is easy in Perugia. Take for instance Via del Paradiso. The least practised eye can spot here that the narrow medieval bricks of the upper storeys rise from massive Etruscan walls. Here too are arches filled in long ago, half-abandoned architraves and crumbly unfinished walls. Parts of the Etruscan walls still survive, notably the great main gateway which Augustus Caesar restored after the Romans took Perugia from the Etruscans in 310 BC, dropping for a time the Etruscan name *Perusia* and substituting *Augusta*.

Perugia's finest era began in the twelfth century and ended in the fifteenth. Money-changers and bankers built the Collegio del Cambio for their trade in the mid fifteenth century. A hundred years later the economy of Perugia was already in decline, partly because of its geographical isolation, partly because the sixteenth century was a time of general economic crisis in Italy, and partly because the different factions within the city fought incessantly until the Baglioni family finally triumphed. The papacy also fought for supremacy, and in 1540 Perugia finally submitted to its sway.

The heart of Perugia is Piazza IV Novembre, marked by a ceremonial fountain which is one of the finest in Italy. Standing on the site of a Roman reservoir, the Fontana

A corner of Siena cathedral.

Maggiore in truth celebrates an aqueduct constructed in the late thirteenth century to bring water to the centre of the city from Monte Pacciano. The fountain was created in 1277 to the designs of the architect of the aqueduct, Fra Bevignate. Boninsegna da Venezia worked out the system of hydraulics, and Nicola and Giovanni Pisano came to sculpt decorative panels and statues. On the lower basin of the fountain the twelve scenes depicting the rustic activities of each month are particularly charming, especially the panel representing April, for which the sculptors depicted a young man and a maiden, he carrying flowers, she laden with fruit. Altogether there are twenty-five panels on this lower basin. As you walk round, two eagles appear. Above the right-hand one Giovanni Pisano added his signature. Symbols of the months of the year, figures from the Old and New Testaments, from classical mythology, from Aesop's fables and from Christian history lie below the bronze female statues on the upper basin of the fountain. Nicola and Giovanni Pisano have here once again brought into the hilltowns of Italy a gothic art that had already flowered across the Alps.

The Fontana Maggiore stands between the cathedral of San Lorenzo and the Palazzo dei Priori. Outside the former a bronze statue created by Vincenzo Danti in 1555 depicts the renaissance Pope Julius III enthroned in St Peter's chair, blessing the young people who sit idly on the steps with their backs towards him. The *duomo* of Perugia is one of those Italian churches that you are glad remains unfaced, the warm stones of its walls pierced with graceful narrow windows. The building is basically gothic, but has been enhanced with renaissance elements, such as the loggia stretching to the right of the statue of the pope, the north door, and the graceful pulpit beside it.

LEFT
Perugia's magnificent medieval town hall, the Palazzo dei Priori, with the Fontana Maggiore in the square between it and the cathedral.

RIGHT
Like many a building in Perugia, this courtyard behind the cathedral beguilingly curves around a corner.

The inlaid choir of 1491 is the masterpiece of Giuliano da Maiano and Domenico del Tasso. And undoubtedly the most curious chapel in the whole cathedral is that in the north aisle which was created to house what the Perugians took to be the wedding ring of the Blessed Virgin Mary. Evidently St Joseph chose onyx to grace the finger of his bride.

The Palazzo dei Priori is one of the city's most complex and yet satisfying buildings, and like the Fontana Maggiore represents the immense civic pride of medieval Perugia. Building began in the late thirteenth century, under the supervision of Giacomo di Servadio and Giovanello di Benvenuto. It finished in 1353, began again in the first half of the fifteenth century and ended only when the loggia and steps facing the great fountain to the east were completed in 1588. The semi-circular flight of steps which bulges out opposite the fountain was added in 1902. Looking at the *palazzo* from the fountain you instantly perceive the genius of the architects in deliberately creating asymmetrical beauty.

The flight of steps leads up to the room of the notaries, once the citizens' assembly hall. Its wide Roman arches and its late thirteenth-century frescoes illustrating tales from Scripture, folklore and legend, by a pupil of Pietro Cavallini, add to the air of magnificence. The *palazzo* faces south onto Corso Vannucci, its gently curving façade setting off the principal entrance which opens onto this street. Two carved griffins, the symbol of Perugia, perch on either side of this portal; each has seized a calf, the symbol of the butchers' guild which paid for most of the *palazzo*. The pillars on which they perch are also allegorically carved, the left one with the figures of avarice, greed and humility, the right one with representations of generosity, fertility and pride. Once again, as in the frescoes of *Good and Evil Government* at Siena, we are confronted with the intense morality of the Middle Ages and the manner in which its art aimed at civilizing the world of business. Three statues in the portico also illustrate the unity of the medieval European world, their worn stone images representing St Louis of Toulouse, the Spanish martyr St Lawrence, and St Ercolano, patron of Perugia, put to death in 547 when the city was betrayed to the Goth Totila.

The Palazzo dei Priori houses the Umbrian national gallery. Even the most cursory gallop through it should take in the sculptures of Arnolfo di Cambio, a couple of Madonnas – one by Giotto, the other by Piero della Francesca – and above all the works of Perugino (Pietro Vannucci) and his follower Bernardino Pintoricchio. Despite his nickname, Vannucci, who lived from 1445 to 1523, was not born in Perugia, but Pintoricchio was a native of the city. Room 15 of the gallery is a cornucopia of their masterpieces, including an extremely moving painting of the dead Jesus by Perugino.

Not far away along Corso Vannucci is the Collegio del Cambio, the seat of the city's guild of money changers. By the thirteenth century, the great industrialists, merchants and bankers of many Italian cities had organized themselves into guilds, whose wealth financed many great buildings and artists of the period. Built in the 1450s, the *collegio* boasts an audience chamber frescoed by Perugino himself as well as a chapel graced by a Madonna painted by his pupil Raphael.

Perugia's merchants and bankers prospered, and the city expanded well after the

Middle Ages. On the west side of Piazza Matteotti rises the noble renaissance Palazzo del Capitano del Popolo, which dates from the 1470s and was designed by two Lombard architects, Gasperino di Antonio and Leone di Matteo. Alongside this palace is the long Tribunali, built between 1472 and 1481 to house the city university, its powerfully arched lower storey contrasting with the grace of the two floors above. On the same side is a covered market, overlooking the shimmering green plain of Assisi. Then the picturesquely stepped Via Sant'Ercolano, which runs down to the polygonal church of the same name, plunges you back into the Middle Ages. Sant'Ercolano was built between 1297 and 1326 on the spot where the saint was martyred, though you enter today by way of a sixteenth-century stairway. Alas for this church, it was partly demolished to make way for the Rocca Paolina, the fortress that was constructed over part of medieval Perugia in the mid-sixteenth century by Pope Paul III, reasserting the

Part of the delicately carved doorway of Perugia's Palazzo dei Priori.

papal authority which the city had defied by refusing to pay the salt tax. Aristotile and Antonio Sangallo who built the fortress included in it an Etruscan gate of the third century BC, the Porta Marzia, which they took down and re-erected 3 metres from its original position. Through this gate you can still gain entrance most mornings to the bizarre subterranean Via Baglione. This symbol of papal domination rankled for the next two centuries. In 1860, when Perugia became part of the kingdom of Italy after a bloody struggle with papal forces, much of the hated Rocca Paolina was torn down.

Monastic orders vied with the guilds in enriching medieval Perugia. The city still boasts the pink-and-white church of San Domenico, which was begun in 1394, though its façade has yet to be finished. Next door the renaissance cloister, once walked by Dominican monks, is now the home of the Umbrian museum of archaeology – an ideal use, it seems to me, for a redundant yet exquisite building. The Benedictines gave

Perugia the monastery and church of San Pietro, whose slender campanile points 75 metres towards heaven. Built on the site of a Roman temple, the building utilizes pagan columns to divide the nave from the aisles of its late sixteenth- and early seventeenth-century interior. The Benedictines were here long before then, and their church houses some fine treasures of earlier times: two stone pulpits by Francesco da Guido, who finished carving them in 1530; sixteenth-century choir-stalls; and canvases by Tiepolo brought here from Venice.

Another side of medieval life is illustrated by Via della Gabbia, which means street of the cage. The name is derived from the medieval Perugians' unkind habit of caging condemned prisoners here and exhibiting them to the crowd. This quarter of Perugia is overlooked by the blank walls of the twelfth-century tower of the Sciri, jutting 46 metres into the sky. Once there were many such towers in the city, known, as this one is, by the names of the ruling families that owned them. The rest have either been demolished or incorporated into later buildings.

If medieval families continually fought and quarrelled with each other, they also managed to come together in religious confraternities that could remain at peace with each other. The oratory of San Francesco in Via degli Sciri is an architectural legacy of this piety. Its full name is the Oratorio della Confraternita dei Disciplinati di San Francesco, for this church once belonged to a confraternity of three different religious orders, Augustinian, Dominican and Franciscan, who came together in Perugia in 1472. A beautifully crafted early baroque church, the oratory boasts a couple of rows of lovely walnut seats and splendid stucco-work by the Frenchman Jean Regnaud de Champagne (who in Italian becomes Giovanni da Sciampagna).

Medieval Perugia was rich enough to rebuild some of its ancient heritage. The Etruscan arch known as the Arco di San Luca (or the Porta Trasimena) near this church, for instance, has not entirely retained its Etruscan aspect, since it was rebuilt with a point in the Middle Ages. Not far away, up the steps leading to Via della Sposa, stand the thirteenth-century church of Sant'Andrea and a genuine medieval gateway, the Porta di Santa Susanna. Through this gate, beyond the medieval walls, the road leads left to the fourteenth-century church of yet another Benedictine convent, Santa Maria della Colombata. The church served the needs of Benedictine nuns until 1437, by which time their morals had become so lax that the community was dissolved.

The red and white façade of Santa Maria della Colombata is charming. Even more so is that of the church of San Francesco al Prato, overlooking the piazza of the same name, with a campanile dating from 1230. Restored in 1926 (the seventh centenary of the founding of the Franciscan order), the façade is a delicate mix of pink and white patterns, relieved with a series of blank arcades. Alas the interior is much changed, not through the folly of succeeding architects but because the unstable ground on which it stands made proper foundations impossible. Deconsecrated, San Francesco al Prato has also lost most of its former treasures, apart from some notable fifteenth-century tombs and a contemporary red stone altar.

To the left of the church stands the oratory of San Bernardino, another Perugian church with a lovely façade. It was begun in 1451, a year after the canonization of St

The astonishing delicacy of the sixth-century interior of Sant'Angelo, Perugia, with a circle of white marble pillars supporting its dome.

Bernardino of Siena whose preaching had made an enormous impact on Perugia in the 1440s. This heroic saint had been born in the Tuscan town of Massa Marittima. Orphaned by the age of seven, he was given such a devout upbringing by his guardians that at the age of seventeen he decided to join a confraternity dedicated to severe self-mortification and the care of the sick. When Siena was visited by the plague in 1400, he took over a hospice for the dying and almost succumbed to the disease himself. Ordained as a priest, he could preach for hours. At the end of his sermons he would hold up a sign bearing the letters IHS (which symbolize Jesus), surrounded by the rays of the sun. When a manufacturer of playing cards complained that St Bernardino's attack on gambling had cost him his living, the saint ordered the man to print copies of the IHS sign, and the printer was soon flourishing again. Such was Bernardino's influence that the 300 friars of the monastic order which he joined in the early fifteenth century had swollen to over 4000 brothers by the time of the saint's death in 1444.

Agostino di Duccio came from Florence to create the magically delicate polychrome façade of San Bernardino at Perugia between 1457 and 1461. At the heart of the façade, in a mandorla at the centre of the tympanum, St Bernardino rises to heaven, welcomed by a band of angelic musicians in flowing robes, while the winged heads of cherubs fly around in rapture. The gothic and much simpler interior houses another relic of Perugia's antiquity, a beautifully preserved and decorated fourth-century Christian sarcophagus which was placed here to serve as the altar in 1494.

Nothing could better illustrate the differences between the major medieval hilltowns of Umbria than the contrast between Perugia and Gubbio. Whereas Perugia straddles two hills, Gubbio simply pours down the side of the Apennines, its streets some of the steepest encountered in Italy. Whereas Perugia's medieval character has to compete against a heritage that is also Etruscan and baroque, Gubbio remains enshrined in one era, its artistic and architectural development virtually halted when the papal state took power here in 1624.

A walk through Gubbio discloses the most varied delights: ancient churches, Roman remains, crumbling walls and narrow streets laid out in the Middle Ages. In the little Largo del Bargello is a fifteenth-century fountain decorated with the five bubbles (or else little round loaves) which form the city's coat of arms. Egubians claim that any persons who run three times round the fountain deserve honorary citizenship of Gubbio, having shown themselves as carefree as children. The fountain's nickname reveals another attitude to such runners: it is known as the Fontana dei Matti, the spring of lunatics.

The Palazzo Ducale and the *duomo* stand side by side near the top of the town. The courtyard of the palace sets the scene, massive Corinthian columns supporting an arcaded loggia on three sides. The whole is topped by a graceful renaissance upper storey, built of pink bricks with delicately carved stone pilasters and architraves. The courtyard is always open, the powerful *palazzo* only part of the time. Well worth a visit, its architecture is in the massy style that became fashionable in Gubbio in the late fifteenth century. It was built to the glory of Duke Federico da Montefeltro, the illegitimate Duke of Urbino who was one of the most distinguished art patrons and ferocious military men of the fifteenth century. His monogram FD (for 'Federicus Dux') appears everywhere here.

The romanesque *duomo* opposite sports a carving of the Lamb of God on its west façade, below which are sculpted the symbols of the four evangelists, with St Mark curiously represented by the figure of a saint, rather than as a winged lion. The interior is a great hall, its roof supported by a succession of pointed brick arches leading towards the gothic apse, with a painted, star-spangled sky covering the high altar. In the centre of the nave is the tombstone of Federico Fregosi, who died in 1541. So many feet have blithely walked over it that his marble features have been scuffed away, and today the cathedral authorities have started defending the marble with a rope barrier. A painting by Raphael's tutor Timoteo Viti on the second altar to the left suggests whence the master may have derived his penchant for chubby cherubs.

Gubbio cathedral boasts many such entertaining paintings, set over altars which enshrine the simple tombs of former bishops. Over the altar next to the painting by Viti, for instance, Sinobaldi Urbi painted a sixteenth-century *Virgin and Saints* which portrays St Sebastian dressed as a renaissance fop, languidly fingering an arrow. A vivid contrast with these unpretentious chapels is the flamboyantly baroque Chapel of the Holy Sacrament on the other side of the cathedral. Bishop Sperelli who built it in the seventeenth century is buried here in a tomb on the right. A wrought-iron screen stops anyone getting in to pray.

Inside the cathedral are many representations of St Ubaldo, sometime bishop of Gubbio and still its patron saint. A little road running around the north side of the cathedral leads up to the medieval gate named after him, Porta Sant'Ubaldo. From it you can enjoy a view of the massive, simple cathedral campanile as well as a prospect over ancient Gubbio and the plain below. The walls either side of the gate, in mint condition, reveal successive stages of building. The lower stones are much bigger and rougher hewn than the upper, though not so massive as, say, those in the walls of Spoleto. And echoing the medieval walls is a stretch of a far less sophisticated and powerful inner ring, the remnant of some earlier defensive system.

Through another medieval gate, the thirteenth-century Porta Romana, is the classical façade of the church of Sant'Agostino. Its interior could be that of the cathedral, save for a plethora of baroque side-chapels. This time the holy of holies is decorated with fifteenth-century frescoes by Ottaviano Nelli, depicting the life of St Augustine. Notice that the cycle does not end with his death. We see the saint borne on a litter for burial, and then he leans out of heaven, still dressed as a bishop, performing miracles and rescuing Christians from prison (while a guard, wearing quaint medieval underpants, sleeps). Ottaviano Nelli also painted a *Last Judgment* on the arch preceding the apse, but it is in poor condition. To the right of the high altar hangs a huge wooden crucifix. Opposite is a classical organ whose caryatids and flanking saints seem slightly indecent in such a devout setting.

The corpse of Bishop Ubaldo watches over the town from the mountain rising behind it. A red brick cloister, remodelled in the renaissance style in 1514 and with a central well, leads into his basilica. St Ubaldo has lain here since 1194, his withered corpse

The mighty ogival arches and the gothic apse of Gubbio cathedral.

dressed in episcopal clothing, his slightly decaying face to my mind less than attractive despite his sanctity. Still, the huge marble catafalque with its mosaics of saints which upholds his glass coffin is impressive enough. Modern stained glass depicts scenes from his life, as well as Pope Honorius II declaring him a saint in 1192, a mere thirty-two years after his death. As Bishop of Gubbio this gentle man was bold enough to confront the Holy Roman Emperor Frederick Barbarossa, who was besieging the town, persuading him to desist and offering the hand of friendship. Today, as well as succouring the faithful, the saint has an active role in one of Gubbio's festivals. Near his corpse you can see three massive candlesticks, rather like huge Christmas crackers. On 15 May, the eve of the anniversary of the saint's death, these *ceri* are carried down to the centre of Gubbio, along with Ubaldo's mortal remains, where they are blessed by the present bishop. Then one candlestick is topped with a statue of the saint himself, a

103

second with a statue of the third-century monk St Anthony Abbot, and a third with a statue of St George. The three *ceri* are affixed to platforms with handles, and then men career through the streets, racing to the cathedral with the saints hoisted in the air.

The medieval way up to the basilica is a cool, winding, sandy road, shaded by cypresses, which loops back and forth across the hill. The monks long ago thought this path up Mount Ingino sufficiently lengthy to keep them unspotted by the world. On 5 July 1944 a member of the Italian resistance was shot on this peaceful road, and the monument where he died records that he was a 'shining example of all Christian virtues'.

An eighteenth-century statue of Ubaldo under a pompous baldacchino in Corso Garibaldi strikes an incongruous note in this most medieval of cities. From either side of the *corso* run narrow medieval streets, those on the right climbing up the hillside, those on the left steeply descending, with many flights of steps and archways tunnelled through houses. To the south along Via Falcucci rises the Porta Vittoria, a double gateway, the interior part with portcullis slits still intact. Hooks that were once used for carrying oil lamps still protrude from one of the houses in Via Reposita. Ahead appear the inner city walls and beyond them rise the octagonal campanile and gothic church of San Francesco, and the long low walls of a convent. Lofty, three-aisled, spacious, the church itself seems unchanged since Fra Bevignate of Perugia built it at the end of the thirteenth century and Ottaviano Nelli frescoed its apse in the fifteenth. The only modern element is the veneration of St Maximilian Kolbe, who died in a Nazi concentration camp, substituting himself for a married prisoner who had been chosen for execution. Across the square is the so-called gallery of the weavers, an impressive arcaded building which once belonged to the most important guild in medieval Gubbio. Its fourteenth-century arches now shelter fruit stalls and bars.

North-west of here, a passageway off Via Cavour leads to the Teatro Romano. Lying outside the city walls, the Roman theatre of Gubbio is small, unlike those of Spoleto or Fiesole. No natural amphitheatre, it was built up artificially and finished in the second century AD. Grass now covers the tiers of seats. Nearby are children's swings. Yet the atmosphere of the site is not domestic but thrilling, with the craggy hills which surround Gubbio providing a dramatic backdrop. Today the Egubians still use the Teatro Romano for open-air drama and ballet.

From here the city rises up the mountainside, a jumble of turrets, towers, palaces and defensive walls. The most prominent building is the square bulk of the Palazzo dei Consoli, its arched openings and windows rising above a fortress-like base, gothic machicolations topping the walls, and a battlemented square tower rising from one corner. Although Angela da Orvieto played his part in designing this magnificent fourteenth-century palace, its colossal scale and the daring of its construction betray the hand of the Umbrian genius Matteo Gattapone. So too do the enormous and characteristic arches which support it and the huge Piazza della Signoria in which the *palazzo* stands. Walk up Via Gattapone on the left side of the *palazzo*, zig-zagging your way to reach the front of the outrageously audacious building. The façade is as disorderly as Gattapone's genius could make it. Today his creation houses Gubbio's

Gubbio, dominated by the castellated Palazzo Pretorio and with the cathedral on the hill above. A stretch of the town's medieval walls can be seen beyond the cathedral.

municipal art gallery, entered by an extremely gracious flight of steps designed by Angela da Orvieto.

Gattapone was also responsible for the Palazzo Pretorio on the other side of the piazza. Although unfinished (he intended it to be twice its present length), it is still stunning – especially inside, where a single octagonal column supports three storeys. When his Palazzo dei Consoli was opened in 1338, that too was unfinished. Nonetheless the Egubians went ahead with their ceremony. They intended their own city to be a new version of ancient Rome, and the celebrations coincided with the anniversary of the founding of Italy's capital. Today the nineteenth-century classical Palazzo Ranghiasci-Branceleoni closes the north side of the square, from where a delightful staircase snakes up the hill under buttresses and arches as far as the Palazzo Ducale and the cathedral. And opposite you can look out over the whole city, across a mosaic of tiled medieval roofs.

That doyen of Italian travel writers, Edward Hutton, thought Siena and Perugia the greatest hilltowns of Tuscany and Umbria respectively. But he went on to single out what he considered a greater one. 'It is true that Perugia looks out over a world famous and holy beyond any other in Italy; it is true that Siena all day long looks on Mont'Amiata, the most beautiful mountain in Tuscany,' he wrote; 'but neither the one nor the other possesses such landscapes as Camerino has in abundance, each and all of which might seem to be a picture by Perugino, full of the largeness and the spaciousness of that master, who alone among the painters of Umbria and Tuscany understood the evening earth, the mystery of sunshine, the opening wonder of the morning, the beauty of the garden of the world.' He regretted that many of its great churches had been taken into secular use, serving as a cinema, as the tramway station, as the local museum. Three-quarters of a century ago he conceded that Camerino seemed 'a little broken down, a little too big for its population, melancholy and dark and full of the moaning wind that fills these narrow streets so often with a rather bitter music'. Yet, for Edward Hutton, Camerino was the queen of all hill cities, guarding the sources of the Chienti.

Dare I disagree with him? Perched 600 metres above sea-level, Camerino does indeed command a splendid site; but I see it as a nineteenth-century vision of a medieval town, and architectural history bears me out. The *duomo* houses several medieval treasures, but an earthquake felled it at the beginning of the nineteenth century and much of it had to be rebuilt. Fourteenth-century San Venanzio was virtually recreated in 1875. Edward Hutton points us to another medieval hilltown in the Marches, Macerata, which I find superior to his favourite. In spite of the fact that today it is a busy modern city, Macerata still stands 'on its great isolated hill piled up upon lesser hills that are covered with gardens of olives, with vineyards and terraces, where the corn waves purple and gold in the July sun'. The trapezoid heart of the town still retains its fourteenth-century walls. Macerata was raised to the status of a city by Pope John XXII in 1320, and its church of San Giuliano became a cathedral. The present building dates from the 1770s, but the campanile is authentically fourteenth century.

To return from the Marches to Umbria is to fall upon a cluster of medieval towns and cities, each offering unrivalled (because unique) riches. Amelia is surrounded by

RIGHT
The hilltown of Amelia.

LEFT
Massive arches shade the pavement near San
Venanzio, Camerino.

107

One figure has disappeared from the late fourteenth-century group of statues depicting the enthronement of the Madonna over the doorway of the basilica of San Venanzio, Camerino. The surviving saint on the Virgin Mary's right is St Porforio.

centuries-old walls pierced by four gates, one of them ornamented with a renaissance portal. This is said to be Umbria's oldest town, founded 3000 years ago by a queen named Ameroe. Parts of its walls were built by the Romans six centuries before the birth of Jesus, and a roman arch now carries renaissance ornamentation as well as a fifteenth-century town-crier's lodging.

Narrow medieval streets climb up to the cathedral past the gothic façade of the fourteenth-century church of Sant'Agostino. The twelve-sided cathedral campanile was built in 1050, the cathedral itself rebuilt in 1640. In San Francesco, Amelia boasts another gothic church which has retained its thirteenth-century façade and rose window. Inside is the tomb which Agostino di Duccio created in 1477 for Matteo and Elisabetta Geraldini, members of one of those powerful Christian families whose loyalty to the papacy did not stop them fighting to preserve their city's independence

A detail from the gothic
doorway of the church of
Sant'Agostino, Amelia.

from the secular power of Rome throughout the Middle Ages.

Gualdo Cattaneo is another such treasure on a hill, with towers jutting from its walls, a church with a thirteenth-century crypt, and a cylindrical tower built by the pope in 1494 to keep the citizens in order. The hilltown of Corciano offers views rivalling those from Macerata and Camerino. Its medieval walls enclose splendidly restored churches and palaces, in particular Santa Maria Assunta whose medieval tower is topped by a belfry of 1864. Nocera Umbra, its white walls and ruined *rocca* surrounded by the trees which cover the upper half of a hillock in the Popino valley, has a fourteenth-century church dedicated to St Francis of Assisi and frescoed by Niccolò Alunno. Christianity came early to Nocera Umbra, traditionally ascribed to the missionary work of the third-century martyr St Feliciano. Its fine cathedral was begun in the eleventh century and then rebuilt in 1448, though the restorers were kind enough to preserve one

LEFT
Via della Corgna, one of the
exquisitely restored streets of
Corciano.

RIGHT
At Nocera Umbra, ancient steps, adorned
with potted plants, rise from Corso Vittorio
Emanuele.

RIGHT
The cathedral belfry and the
eleventh-century tower of the
Trinci dominate the skyline
of Nocera Umbra.

romanesque doorway. Its sacristy boasts a decorated majolica pavement.

Panicale is another beguiling Umbrian hilltown that as yet has escaped most guidebooks, even though it plunges visitors back into the Middle Ages. Its collegiate church, its asymmetrical, sloping squares, the dark stones of its thirteenth-century Palazzo Podestà snooze inside medieval walls, while outside them a couple of frescoes by Perugino adorn the church of San Sebastiano. Montefalco perhaps outstrips these lesser, albeit entirely satisfying medieval Umbrian hilltowns, if only because its virtually circular central piazza is so gorgeous as well as intimate. The Palazzo Comunale dominates without stifling the rest of the buildings. The former church of San Francesco, dating back to the fourteenth century, is now an art gallery with just enough paintings and sculptures from the Middle Ages to satisfy without tiring the visitor. The views from the 471-metre hill on which Montefalco is built are so

Panicale's renaissance well.

OVERLEAF LEFT
A mullioned window of the eleventh-century church of San Bartolomeo at Montefalco.

exceptional as to have earned it the soubriquet 'the balcony of Umbria'. The church of San Bartolomeo injects a flavour of the romanesque into the predominantly gothic architecture, so that here we can readily compare the distinctiveness of the two styles. From San Bartolomeo's apse, Viale Federico II leads to the medieval church of Santa Chiara which houses frescoes painted in the 1330s, while the street leading from the central square towards the Porta Federico II, which was built in 1244, passes the exquisite, tiny thirteenth-century church of Santa Lucia. And Montefalco also beguiles the visitor by means of its gently soporific red wine.

South towards Sicily, the medieval inheritance becomes more complex, reflecting more varied influences. The hilltown of Enna, for example, benefitted from the foreign rulers of this region, the Hohenstaufen dynasty and its successor the house of Aragon. The massive Hohenstaufen fortress here is partly Byzantine, partly Norman and also, in

A blocked-up window of the church of San Bartolomeo, by the Porta Federico in Montefalco.

OVERLEAF RIGHT
The tiled roofs of Montefalco, seen from the tower of the Palazzo Comunale.

its impressive use of monumental walls, partly Swabian in style, for the Hohenstaufens ruled the duchy of Swabia from 1079. Then, in the fourteenth century, Frederick III of Aragon extensively rebuilt the fortress with the sumptuousness which crowned medieval architecture in this region at that time. Once it boasted twenty towers. Six remain. Of the *castello's* three courtyards, that known as Santa Nicola is now an open-air theatre seating 8000 spectators.

The curves of Via Roma lead from here to the cathedral. Though partly transformed in the sixteenth century, and in spite of the dark Corinthian columns which support the interior, its gothic transept and apses still bear witness to the artistry of the original fourteenth-century builders. Beyond are the remains of the fifteenth-century Palazzo Pollicarini, half-gothic, half-Catalan in style, and mixed architectural influences are again revealed by the former church of San Giovanni Battista, with an Arabic cupola crowning its gothic, three-tier campanile. As for medieval spirituality, this is proclaimed by the greatest treasure of the church of San Francesco in Piazza Vittorio Emanuele: a painted wooden crucifixion, contemporary with the fifteenth-century campanile if not even earlier.

Religion, as we have already seen, played a central role in the flowering of the Middle Ages. The devout citizens of medieval Enna gathered together in fourteen religious confraternities, the oldest dating back to 1261. These survive to this day. During Holy Week their members process through the city, dressed in their ancient costumes. In these rituals the Middle Ages live again. Membership of a medieval guild usually carried the obligation to take part in such celebrations. At Enna the rites culminate in a Good Friday procession in which statues of the weeping Virgin Mary and the cadaver of her dead son are borne from church to church and finally to the cathedral.

One of the delights of visiting Enna is to see the superb view of the countryside around and of Mount Etna from the 931-metre peak on which it is built, the finest panoramas rewarding those who climb the so-called Pisan tower of the Castello di Lombardia. The Greek poet Callimachus dubbed this place 'the navel of Sicily'. Cicero gave the city a politer name: 'Sicily's belvedere'. Enna was thought to be impregnable. Nonetheless, in 951 the Saracens attempted to capture the city. Across the motorway to the north you can see the horseshoe-like fortress they built on a neighbouring peak. Known today as Calascibetta (from the Arabic 'Kalat-Scibet'), its church of San Pietro adds a fourteenth-century Christian element to a town created by the Moors. Its interior consists of ogival arches supported by pillars whose bases carry sculpted monsters. In the sixteenth century Capuchin monks also built a church at Calascibetta; inside is a noted retable created by F. Paladino in 1613, illustrating the Adoration of the Magi.

The surviving towers of Enna's Castello di Lombardo bring to mind Tuscany's medieval gem. If Gubbio is more satisfyingly homogeneous than Perugia, San Gimignano al Monte in Tuscany is even more all of a piece. Until 1348 the town prospered and expanded, benefitting from a lucrative trade in saffron and wine and from its position on the pilgrimage route from Lombardy to Rome. Via Giovanni and Via S. Matteo, which lead past the cathedral, trace the ancient pilgrimage route, the late eleventh-century Templars' church which still stands here recalling the pilgrims'

The renaissance portal of Enna cathedral was sculpted by Gian Domenico Gagini in 1560 and depicts St Martin slicing his cloak in two to give one half to a naked beggar.

hostels founded by the Knights Templars and the Knights of Malta. For a time the great nobles of the town vied with each other for control of the city, building themselves gaunt towers – status symbols, granaries and fortresses – from which they could sally forth to inflict wounds on their enemies. Of the original thirty-six, thirteen still remain, bizarre medieval skyscrapers, some of them twinned, others carrying a little belfry or topped with a decorative pinnacle, but most of them nowadays supporting nothing but vegetation.

The twelfth century found the merchants of San Gimignano in every great city of Europe. Yet the commercial prosperity of this and the next century failed to soften the feudal spirit of its great families. Obsessed with fighting each other, the people of San Gimignano also warred against the neighbouring towns and cities of Tuscany, supporting Florence against Siena, Arezzo and Volterra. In the early thirteenth

century, led by the Salvucci family, the citizens took the side of the Ghibellines (supporters of the Holy Roman Emperor) against the Guelphs (supporters of the papacy), changing allegiances in 1269 when the Ardighelli family gained the upper hand. Such a warlike people needed to protect themselves: no fewer than three successive rings of walls were built around the city as the Middle Ages progressed, the first in the eleventh century, the next in 1236, and the final ring in 1262 after the Florentines had demolished the defences constructed twenty-six years earlier.

As the fourteenth century opened, a new era of even greater prosperity dawned. Five new convents sprang up. Rich citizens established a foundling hospital. Giacomo da Michele, a poet who flourished between 1309 and 1317 and took the name Folgòre da San Gimignano, hymned the luxury of his age:

> *Di maggio si vi do molti cavagli*
> *e tutti quanti siano affrenatori,*
> *portanti tutti, dritti corritori,*
> *pettorali e testiere con sonagli;*
> *bandiere e coverte a molti 'ntagli*
> *di zendadi e di tutti li colori,*
> *le targhe a modo degli armeggiatori,*
> *viole rose e fior c'ogni uon abbagli.*

> For the month of May I give you many horses,
> all of them manageable, all of them properly broken,
> their riders sitting upright,
> bells hanging from their breastplates and head-dresses,
> flags, and silken, multi-coloured trappings,
> jousters' shields, as well as violets, roses
> and other flowers dazzling the crowd.

In 1348 the Black Death transformed this splendour into misery. As well as reducing the population of the city to perhaps a third of what it was, the plague also ensured that pilgrims no longer stopped to rest here. Five years later, the town humiliatingly submitted to the rule of Florence. A century later pestilence again cut down its citizens. Only the convents continued to thrive, supported by the fellow monasteries elsewhere in Italy. Thus the scourge of the Middle Ages preserved San Gimignano as if in amber. In 1563 the Medicis of Florence forbade any more building here, a scarcely necessary ordinance, since the economy of the town lay in ruins. In consequence, to this day San Gimignano remains an extravagantly improbable thirteenth- and fourteenth-century Italian hilltown. On any visit, as Henry James put it, the town seems like a friendly, buried, heroic skeleton, positively waking up to show you his bones for a fee.

A spacious garden laid out in 1875 outside the Porta San Giovanni marks the site of the foundling hospital. The gate itself was fortified in the sixteenth century on the orders of Cosimo I de' Medici, who feared that the Sienese were about to attack his dependency. He also built the massive round bastion that fortifies the outer walls.

Craggy Calascibetta, seen from Enna.

OVERLEAF
The characteristic silhouette of San Gimignano, its medieval towers like soaring skyscrapers.

Two of the arrogant medieval
towers of San Gimignano.

Today, however, the gateway has been restored to what it was like in 1262. Beyond it is the shady medieval Via San Giovanni, where a former Franciscan convent boasting a calm romanesque façade was once occupied by the Knights of Malta. Today you can buy wine here, especially the gorgeous white Vernaccia dï San Gimignano, and enjoy a view of the rolling countryside beyond the walls. The street is also lined with the gothic palaces of the former nobles, one of them, the former palace of the Pratellesi family, now the city library. As well as a modern collection, it houses an astonishing legacy of 10,000 manuscripts and 35,000 ancient books. The palace itself is a treat, with double-mullioned gothic windows and trefoiled terracotta arches. The main hall of the library was delicately frescoed by Raphael's pupil Vincenzo Tamagni, a native of the town.

Via San Giovanni debouches into the utterly enchanting, triangular Piazza della Cisterna. Over the centuries the chains on which buckets were let down to fetch water

122

from the thirteenth-century well here have gouged grooves in its crumbling stones. What makes the square one of the glories of San Gimignano is the diverse architecture of the palaces surrounding it: the red bands of brick and the sophisticated pointed windows of the fourteenth-century Palazzo Tortoli offer a particularly piquant contrast to the older, pitted stones of the other palaces, with blank towers rising mutely behind. In the evening, the warm lights of wine shops and bars flood out into the piazza. One of my happiest memories is of staying in the excellent hotel in this square and rising one February morning to find everything covered in a light coating of snow.

Via del Castello leads east from this piazza, shaded by elegant houses and *palazzi*, nearly every one enclosing a courtyard with its own well. This street more than any other in San Gimignano exhibits the town's policy, unusual in medieval Italy, of allowing its citizens to build in any style that appealed to them, those of Lucca or Pisa or Siena or Florence juxtaposing in continually pleasing singularity until you reach the romanesque church of San Lorenzo in Ponte. Built in 1240, it was frescoed in the early fourteenth century by the Sienese master Simone Martini. His finest work in this church (albeit much repainted in subsequent centuries) depicts an angel choir welcoming the Madonna into heaven. Her infant son is playing with a pet bird. Although the frescoes in this church by other hands are fine, notably a sequence depicting the life of St Benedict, none matches the skill of Martini's *Assumption*. Just when you decide that every angel is rather cloyingly gazing at the Blessed Virgin, you spot that one of them playing a kind of squeeze-box has brought an enhanced rhythm to the fresco by turning away from the two central figures.

A few paces north-west of the Piazza del Cisterna is the religious heart of San Gimignano, the Piazza del Duomo, dominated by the simple, though asymmetrical romanesque front of the former cathedral, built at the behest of Pope Vittore II in 1056 and consecrated by Eugenius III in 1148. Now known as the Collegiata, it rises over equally simple but perfectly judged flights of steps designed by Ranieri da Colle in 1299. The church boasts quite extraordinary frescoes in a town filled with remarkable examples of this art. Those in the north aisle, depicting scenes from the Old Testament, are by Bartolo di Fredi. The ones in the south aisle, with scenes from the New Testament, are by Barna da Siena and his pupil Giovanni d'Ascanio (who was obliged to finish the work when his master fell to his death from the scaffolding). Although the massacre of the innocents in this cycle is entrancingly grisly, undoubtedly the most savage frescoes in the Collegiata are those by the early fifteenth-century Sienese painter Taddeo di Bartolo, depicting the martyrdom of St Sebastian (arrows neatly placed, among other painful spots, in his groin) and devils ferociously torturing the damned.

In the mid fifteenth century Giuliano da Maiano added a renaissance chapel, dedicated to St Fina, patroness of San Gimignano. Scenes from the life of this decidedly weedy saint, a medieval anorexic who starved herself to death at the age of fifteen, were painted here, in settings that have scarcely changed, by Domenico Ghirlandaio and his assistants. The towers of San Gimignano, views of the Tuscan countryside, succulent pomegranates and carafes of wine attend the dying virgin. E. M. Forster, who set his novel *Where Angels Fear to Tread* in San Gimignano and there refers to St Fina as Santa

Deodata, sardonically describes the Ghirlandaio fresco which depicts her 'dying in full sanctity, upon her back'. He wrote: 'There was a window open behind her, revealing just such a view as he had seen that morning, and on her widowed mother's dresser there stood just another copper pot. The saint looked neither at the view nor at the pot, and at her widowed mother still less. For lo! she had a vision: the head and shoulders of St Augustine were sliding like some miraculous enamel along the roughcast wall. It is a gentle saint who is content with half another saint to see her die. In her death, as in her life, Santa Deodata did not accomplish much.'

Forster was not absolutely accurate, since the saint sliding along the wall is Pope Gregory the Great and not Augustine. In the same chapel seek out especially another fresco: that of St Fina lying on her bier before an altar. On the left are a bishop and a server. Behind them the artists (Domenico Ghirlandaio, his brother David and his brother-in-law Sebastiano Mainardi) have painted self-portraits, as if they too were at her funeral. Thus late fifteenth-century artists have put themselves into a painting of a medieval funeral which miraculously reflects the San Gimignano of today. Ghirlandaio performed the same trick in the open-air baptistery on the south side of the Collegiata, painting an *Annunciation* with the Virgin Mary and the Angel Gabriel in a room whose window looks out onto the cypresses still so characteristic of Tuscany. You can see this very landscape from the tower of the nearby Palazzo Comunale, now the city art gallery, which is crammed with masterpieces (the most entrancing of which are the so-called 'profane' frescoes painted in the fourteenth century by Memmo di Filipuccio). As for the rest of San Gimignano's artistic treasures, no one should miss Lippo Memmi's *Maestà*, painted in 1317, or the *Madonna with Saints* by Pintoricchio.

Every twist of the city's streets guides you towards a new gothic treat. Immediately west of the Collegiata is San Gimignano's ruined fourteenth-century fortress, the *rocca*, its sometime fierceness now tamed into a public park. Taking another direction, Via San Matteo leads to the Palazzo del Podestà, built in 1239 and gothicized in 1337, and with the tallest tower in the city. Close by rise the double-towered, thirteenth-century Palazzo Salvucci, the huge Palazzo-Torre Broge Pasciolini of the same date and the romanesque church of San Bartolo. On its lintel is engraved a Maltese cross. Beyond the Porta San Matteo is the Piazza Sant'Agostino and the thirteenth-century church from which it takes its name. Here splendid frescoes painted by Benozzo Gozzoli in the mid 1460s depict seventeen scenes from the life of St Augustine, beginning with the saint as a schoolboy being birched by his master. And a superb panel over the high altar showing the Blessed Virgin, strangely etiolated, being crowned in heaven, was executed by Piero del Pollaiuolo, who signed and dated it in 1483.

Late gothic frescoes can be disquieting. In the chapel of St Bartolo is a painting representing the saint to whom this town is dedicated, Gimignano, holding a model of San Gimignano in the folds of his robe. Sebastiano Mainardi painted him here in 1500. Beside him is a representation of St Lucy. A dagger protrudes from her bleeding neck. Medieval hilltowns, however charming, always preserve a hint of menace.

# 4

# FROM FORTRESS
# TO PALACE

FEDERICO DA MONTEFELTRO (1422–82) is known to every lover of the paintings of Piero della Francesca, if only because the artist was obviously fascinated by the hooked nose of his subject and in a portrait of 1465 (now in the Uffizi, Florence) encapsulated perfectly the implacably determined face of his ducal patron. Federico was not born with such a nose, for it was created at a stroke during a tournament, the same blow slicing out the duke's right eye. The wrinkles, warts and sprouting hair are by contrast authentic works of nature. In the Uffizi the duke stares unblinkingly at his unsmiling long-nosed wife, Battista Sforza, the brocade of whose dress bespeaks his munificence to this twenty-year-old cold beauty. On the reverse of this diptych they drive towards each other, his chariot drawn by white horses, hers by the unicorns that in medieval bestiaries symbolized virginity. What can Piero be saying to us? Federico is accompanied by the four cardinal virtues of justice, prudence, fortitude and temperance. Battista's companions are the three theological virtues, faith, hope and charity. Behind them are displayed panoramas of the duke's domains, with the lakes and hills shrouded in mellow mist.

The artist evidently dared signal the differing virtues of each of his sitters (and perhaps both were pleased to find their characters so sharply delineated). Latin verse underneath Battista's portrait extols her virtues as a woman; that accompanying Federico's portrait speaks only of his triumphs.

The Montefeltro family became lords of the city and duchy of Urbino towards the end of the twelfth century, and throughout the next 400 years skilfully increased their own prosperity and that of their domain. Federico, *condottiere* and determined enemy of the lord of Rimini, Sigismondo Malatesta (who murdered three of his own wives and was defeated by Federico in 1463), was also rich and enlightened enough to become the perfect example of a renaissance patron of art. It is said that he rode into battle reading Herodotus. It is certain that Latin histories were read at meals in his palace, save in Lent, when spiritual works were substituted.

Urbino under Federico became a renaissance city, an expression of that rebirth of classical ideals which began in Italy in the fourteenth century. Art, as Michaelangelo's pupil Giorgio Vasari put it, seemed then to have died and been born again, 'reaching the perfection of our own times'. Classical ideals, the views of newly acclaimed ancients, and along with all this a new form of architecture became the norm. The glorification of humanity was the aim of those who built these towns and cities. The foot, the trunk and the head of a human being now determined the very proportions of the base, the shaft and the capital of a column. As Erwin Panofsky put it, whereas medieval architecture preaches Christian humility and a gothic cathedral forces us to remain conscious of our actual stature in contrast with the size of the building, renaissance architecture now proclaimed the dignity of man.

Piero della Francesca was by no means the only master to flock to Federico's court and enjoy his commissions. Luca Signorelli, Justus of Ghent, Paolo Uccello, the Spaniard Pedro Berrugiete and Titian himself were drawn to the extraordinary prince. One of the most sensuous nudes ever painted was done for the court by Titian, and although today she hangs in the Uffizi, the painting is still justly called the *Venus of Urbino*.

A city that fostered art also bred geniuses who decided to follow painting, sculpture and architecture as their chosen professions. It was here that the architect Donato Bramante was born in 1544, and the painter Federico Barocci in *c*.1535. Giovanni Santi worked for the fifteenth-century court of Urbino as both a painter and a writer. In Giorgio Vasari's celebrated *Lives of the Artists* (1550), Santi is described as 'a mediocre painter but an intelligent man'. He was undoubtedly an assiduous courtier. In twenty-three books of verse Santi lauded the achievements of the Montefeltros, including their generous support for artists, presenting the book to Federico's son Guidobaldo. Guidobaldo's court in turn was celebrated in the renowned book *Il Cortegiano*, a manual for courtiers, written by Castiglione in 1528, twenty years after Guidobaldo's death. Castiglione's masterpiece outlines the humanist ideals encapsulated by the city of Urbino, ideals based on the triumphs of ancient Rome and ancient Greece, a striving both in the human frame and in architecture for what the writer called 'strength, lightness and suppleness'.

In 1483 Santi's son was born, baptized Raffaello Sanzio. He was an architect as well as a painter. We know him as Raphael. Although Vasari asserted that 'Raphael became of great assistance to his father in the many works that Giovanni executed for the state of Urbino', the boy was in truth only eleven years old when his father died. What Raphael surely learned both from Giovanni Santi and the culture of Urbino in general was the humanism which so informs the masterpieces of the High Renaissance which he was to paint in his short thirty-seven years. The house where he was born in Urbino has become a museum, the Casa di Raffaello. There you are shown a little fresco of the Virgin and Child. Some say it is one of Raphael's earliest works. I prefer a rival judgement, namely that this lovely work is a portrait by Giovanni Santi himself of his wife and their infant son.

Lying in the northernmost part of the Marches where the Apennines slope down towards the Adriatic, Urbino, as its name indicates, stands on two hills between the rivers Metauro and Foglia (the Latin *Urbs bina* literally means 'double town'). Although the sea breezes from the east can sweep its streets, to the west Urbino is sheltered by the Apennines. The essayist Michel de Montaigne visited the city a year before Federico died and described it as 'built on a mountain of medium height, but for the most part lying on its slopes, so that you never find a level spot to walk on'. The

The colossal apse of the cathedral of Urbino towers over the hilltown.

128

medieval quarter of Urbino demonstrates the truth of what he wrote. Narrow alleyways and passages twist steeply under archways and turn without warning into steps. Yet although the nineteenth-century poet Giovanni Pascoli affectionately called his birthplace the windy city, the tall, brown brick buildings which flank these winding little roads have effectively sheltered generations of citizens from the sea breezes.

On this medieval city, the descendant of the Roman municipium Urvinum Mataurense, Federico da Montefeltro detemined to impose a state rationally organized according to the ideals of humanism. The symbol of his ideal was to be a castle that should embody in its architecture not the fierceness of a defensive and offensive fortress but the ambience of renaissance civilization. He wanted a palace where civilized men and women could gather to share and consolidate the self-consciously new values of his era. The result was Urbino's superb Palazzo Ducale, a building once described by the art historian Kenneth Clark as 'that pure expression of the finest humanism, in its reason, harmony and light'.

Federico was building his beloved new palace when Piero della Francesca was at Urbino, and a surviving letter written by the master claims he was the duke's trusted adviser in all matters of art. The construction of the Palazzo Ducale, in spite of a total lack of documentary proof, convinced Kenneth Clark that he advised on this. 'Walking through the palace we are everywhere aware of the perfect balance between richness and severity, between delicate detail and simplicity of surface, between space condensed and space expanded, which is characteristic of Piero's architecture as we know it from his paintings.' Having made that assessment Clark judiciously continued, 'we must grant that the beautiful arcaded courtyard by which the palace is best known has no parallel in Piero's work.'

Although not every building in the area of the palace is renaissance, the heart of Urbino is nonetheless a complex piece of renaissance urban design, where the buildings surrounding both Piazza Duca Federico and also the Piazza Rinascimento seem all of a piece. Across the street from Federico's palace you can today sit outside a restaurant and gaze across at the classical cathedral. Its very existence speaks of the vanity of human ambition, for a previous cathedral, inevitably built on the orders of Duke Federico (and superseding an eleventh-century romanesque church), collapsed during the earthquake of 1789. The façade of the present building was constructed in Furlo stone by Camillo Morigia. Beside it rises the eighteenth-century campanile. Giuseppe Valadier designed the rest of the cathedral, which seems to me to pulsate with all the vigour of the Renaissance. Treasures fill its chapels. For the second altar of the right aisle Federico Barocci painted a maryrdom of St Sebastian in which the sole executioner aims an arrow precisely at his navel and the saint swoons voluptuously, his skirts swirling with ecstasy and revealing his flashy underwear. Those who regret the disappearance of the earlier cathedral can console themselves by admiring the wrought-iron grille which guards the Chapel of the Blessed Sacrament, a fifteenth-century work of art rescued from the ruins after the earthquake. Barocci's work is also displayed in the cathedral museum, together with liturgical vestments in rich reds and greens.

Proud prelates, sculpted on the *duomo* of Urbino.

The university, housed in the former Palazzo Bonaventura where the Montefeltros lived till their ducal palace was finished, also overlooks the Piazza Ducale. The façade is inscribed STVDIORVM VNIVERSITATE FASTIGIVM, a motto that could well describe the ambitions of Federico himself. A count till he was elevated to his dukedom in 1474, this restless man devoted his long life to extending his domains and promoting his influence.

Apart from the gothic doorway, the Montefeltros would recognize nothing of their previous home, for the university was almost entirely rebuilt in the seventeenth century. Yet ghosts from the past still hover around. As an inscription on the façade records, in the sixteenth century the poet Torquato Tasso stayed here as a guest of the count. Deeply in love with a courtly lady named Laura Peperara, he wrote sonnets still eloquent of immortal hopes:

132

*Ore, dermate il volo*
*nel lucido oriente,*
*mentre se 'n vola il ciel rapidamente;*
*e, crolando intorno*
*a l'alba mattutina*
*ch'esce de la marina,*
*l'unamana vita ritardate e 'l giorno*

Stay your flight in the luminous east, you hours,
 though heaven flies swiftly on;
and as you dance around the morning light which rises
    from the waves,
slow down human life and the day itself.

I imagine that his soul still flickers somewhere in the shade of this piazza.

The east end of Palazzo Bonaventura boasts an elegance comparable with any other renaissance masterpiece, its superimposed loggias and twin towers suggesting precisely the air of civilized humanism that Federico demanded. These towers make no more than a pretence at self-defence, while the loggias became more delicate as they rise, without ever teetering over into extravagance. Begun in 1444 by Maso di Bartolomeo, the character of the whole building derives above all from the designs of Luciano Laurana who worked on it between 1466 and 1472, incorporating into his overall scheme a couple of existing gothic palaces. He it was who oversaw the masters employed to contribute the details: Barocci for the doors and windows, Domenico Rosselli and Giorgio Martini for sculpted embellishment. Finally, after the death of Federico and a brief respite in his ambitious scheme, the sixteenth-century architect Girolamo Genga completed the upper storeys.

A walk around the building reveals something of its history. From the Piazza del Rinascimento you view the original gothic palace. Walk on into Piazza Duca Federico and you are still confronted with a slightly forbidding castle. Only when you enter the main courtyard does the fortress really transform itself into an elegant palace. Here, a statue of Federico designed by Barocci and sculpted by G. Campagna in 1604 dominates a monumental staircase, providing a focal point for the whole composition.

The portico of Luciano Laurana's orderly renaissance courtyard is surmounted by an entablature whose inscription inevitably praises the achievements of Federico. In translation it reads, 'Duke Federico of Urbino, count of Montefeltro and Casteldurante, gonfalonier of the Holy Roman Church and supreme head of the Italic confederation, raised this house to glorify himself and his descendants. Continually venturing to war, he six times battled against and eight times conquered his enemy, emerging victor from his wars and increasing the greatness of his power. In times of peace, justice and mercy, liberality and faith tempered and enhanced his victories.'

Some of the palace's most splendid rooms are now used to house the national gallery of the Marches. Through a massive throne room (the largest room in the palace), you enter the first of the ducal apartments. Known as the angels' room because of the *putti* which fly around its chimney, this room has superb inlaid doors by Rossellino, who also designed the fireplace. More marquetry work, this time designed by Botticelli and including a delightful *trompe l'oeil* squirrel stealing nuts, enhances the next room, the ducal study (or *studiolo*). So the treats unfold: the rooms of Battista Sforza; another salon filled with sculptures; a third exquisitely frescoed. Giovanni Bellini is represented in the gallery by a *Madonna and Child*, who are flanked by the mother of Mary and St John the baptist. Piero della Francesca's works here include a curious *Flagellation* and his *Madonna de Senegallia*. I describe the *Flagellation* as curious because Jesus is scarcely being beaten and he and his tormentors are unduly subordinate to three figures in the foreground. Scholars have conjectured that one of these, a fair-haired youth, is none other than Oddantonio da Montefeltro, who was murdered, and that Piero was attempting to assimilate his grisly fate with that of Jesus himself. As for his Madonna, all four figures in this painting, baby Jesus, his mother and the two angels, seem to be in a foul temper.

There are many other masterpieces in what remains a comparatively neglected Italian gallery, almost as if the great artists of renaissance Italy dutifully lined up to portray the crucial moments in the passion of Jesus: Luca Signorelli with his pictures of the Crucifixion and the day of Pentecost, Titian with his *Last Supper* and *Resurrection*, Andrea del Verocchio with his *Madonna and Child* and Paolo Uccello with his *Profanation of the Sacred Host*. John Ruskin averred that Uccello 'went off his head with love of perspective', and certainly he exults in depicting vistas in this fifteenth-century strip cartoon in which a sinful woman is hanged and the entire family of an erring merchant burned at the stake. In Federico Barocci's *Assumption*, Mary stands on a crescent moon which resembles a banana. In his *Madonna and Child*, the Blessed Virgin is teaching her child to read. Raphael has contributed his beautiful portrait of a lady who could not speak, *La Muta*. She gazes at us dumbly from the canvas, still an object of desire, her hands placidly crossed. Finally, look out for two portraits of Federico himself. Around 1470 Justus of Ghent painted *The Institution of the Eucharist*. Although not one of the twelve apostles, Federico is present (after all, he did attend Mass every day), wearing his customary red pill-box hat, his hooked nose well displayed, his right hand expressively extended in adoration. A more splendid portrait by Pedro Berruguete depicts Federico with his son Guidobaldo. Although the duke has already handed Guidobaldo his sceptre and is busy reading, he is still armour-clad, ready to take up the role of *condottiere* at a moment's notice.

An enamelled terracotta of the *Virgin Mary surrounded by Saints*, by Luca della Robbia, once adorned the late fourteenth-century church of San Domenico in the Piazza del Rinascimento. The tympanum from which it comes is part of the portal which Duke Federico commisioned from Tomase Bartolomeo in 1450, to enliven the narrow red brick of the dignified façade. In front of the church is an unexpected sight – an Egyptian obelisk carved with hieroglyphics, the gift of Cardinal Albano, a distinguished son of the city, in the eighteenth century.

Everyone should find time in Urbino to visit the Casa di Raffaello. As well as the little fresco I have already mentioned (which hangs in the upstairs room where Santi's son

LEFT
Cobbled streets and
crumbling walls: Via della
Rocca in Soriano nel Cimino.

RIGHT
Italian domesticity revealed in a balcony
overlooking the Piazza Principe di Napoli,
Ronciglione.

was born), the house is decked not only with original drawings by Raphael but also with judiciously chosen reproductions of his work from other parts of Italy. The courtyard is charming. Over a square stone is a plaque which avows 'Su questa pietra venivano macinati i colori nella bottega di Giovanni Santi.' I flatly refuse to believe that the red, white, green, yellow and blue paints so studiously colouring the top of this stone derive from Santi's habit of grinding his paints here.

This part of Urbino is still a defensive city, in spite of the ambitions of Federico da Montefeltro. Via Bramante, for instance, is guarded by the stern sixteenth-century Palazzo Albani, while the panoramic Viale Bruno Buozzi takes you to another austere fortress, the fifteenth-century Fortezza Albornoz, a reminder of the time when Urbino became subject to the papal states.

Since 1981 Urbino has been vigorously promoting itself and its rich history by hosting each August a Festival of Duke Federico Montefeltro, with jousting and costumed parades. Neighbouring Italian cities have been persuaded to compete in the tourney, the winner awarded a banner or *palio*. I relish such festivals, but Urbino in my view needs no promotion.

In spite of the overwhelmingly enticing vision of Federico, renaissance Urbino never managed to erase its medieval forebear. The pattern is repeated again and again in Italian hilltowns and, indeed, provides them with a specially complex enchantment. Often you can see the whole town quietly transforming itself from medieval defensiveness to palatial renaissance or even baroque expansiveness. Take Ronciglione, built on a peak 441 metres above sea-level not quite 20 kilometres from Viterbo on the way to Rome. Lying on the southern slopes of a wooded, once volcanic hill, it boasts the romanesque church of Santa Maria dell Provvidenza, whose tower is of the utmost simplicity. Its apse seems to have skewed a little since the church was built over six centuries ago. The colours of the frescoed Virgin Mary, dressed in a blue robe and a red dress, are still fresh and delicate. Only an ornately incongruous baroque altar with marbled pillars mars the ancient calm of the church.

The medieval town winds down the hillside, a mesh of higgledy-piggledy houses, grey walls, arches and balconies. The cathedral square in the upper town offers an architectural transformation. Even the remains of a medieval fortress with a couple of round towers and a sixteenth-century fountain decorated with unicorns' heads cannot blunt the impact of Carlo Rainaldi's baroque *duomo*. Impressive enough from the outside, but not overly so, with stone torches rising above Doric and Corinthian columns, its interior is overwhelming. Massy Tuscan half-columns supporting the walls, the exquisite throne and cupola, a magnificent baroque altar beyond the pulpit rivalled only by the high altar with its daring use of odd angles and curious curves – all combine to excite the eye and heart.

Soriano nel Cimino presents the same spine-tingling transition as Ronciglione, save that it does so in reverse, with the medieval quarter on the hill above and the sixteenth-century part below. If anything, the spur on which it stands is even more densely wooded than that of Ronciglione, so that the town rises picturesquely from walnuts and chestnut trees. The medieval town is dominated by Castello Orsini, still in splendid

condition, even though it was last altered in 1279. In contrast, the lower town is overlooked by the elegant Palazzo Chigi Albani, built in the mid sixteenth century to the designs of Giacomo Barazzi da Vignola. The terrace of this palace is graced with a remarkable mannerist creation, a fountain known as the Papacqua (though it is sometimes also called the Queen of Fountains).

Even the smallest hilltowns often blossomed in the atmosphere of the Renaissance. Castiglione del Lago, for instance, rises on a promontory overlooking Umbria's largest lake, Lago Trasimeno. The lower town at the foot of the hill is a popular waterside resort, a world apart from the medieval town perched up above, which is enriched by a medieval castle, the Palazzo Ducale della Corgna (or Comunale) which Giovanni Alessi built in the sixteenth century, and the Palazzo Ducale built by Giacomo Barozzi da Vignola in the same era. In the former palace, the rooms are decorated with sixteenth-

**LEFT**
One of the bizarre figures on the Papacqua fountain in Soriano nel Cimino.

**RIGHT**
The narrow entrance to the castle of Castiglione del Lago.

century frescoes, probably by Giovanni Antonio Pandolfi of Pisa and Salvio Savini of Florence.

Despite its somewhat ponderous nineteenth-century classical renovation, the church of La Maddalena is also worth a visit, to admire a painting of the Virgin and Child flanked by St Anthony Abbot and St Mary Magdalene, executed by Perugino's pupil Eusebio da San Giorgio in 1500. Architecturally, I prefer the seventeenth-century church of San Domenico, whose ceiling was superbly decorated a hundred years later. A low, grey crenellated curtain wall, with turrets jutting up from time to time, protects all these treasures.

St Francis of Assisi made a memorable impact here in the thirteenth century when a local fisherman offered him a pike and the saint instantly threw it back into the lake. It was Lent and the emaciated Francis had decided to survive for forty days on only two

Barley grows in the lush pastures around Lake Trasimeno.

loaves of bread. Such abstinence is not expected of visitors, who can enjoy fresh fish from the lake and the pungent fish soup known as *brodetto*. Lake Trasimeno was historically resonant even before the days of St Francis. Reclaimed from the marshes by the Etruscans, its borders were settled by the Romans, who were savagely defeated nearby by Hannibal in 217 BC. Much fought over in the early Middle Ages, the lake continued to remain an area of conflict because until the nineteenth century it lay amid strategic border country. It finally became part of the newly established kingdom of Italy in 1860 when all the surrounding towns and villages voted to join.

Today boats peacefully ply the lake and its islands, taking tourists to restaurants where fish is cooked on open fires fuelled by the reeds which fringe the water and the gorse bushes of the countryside. Another hilltown, Castel Rigone, also boasts a stunning view of the waters of Lake Trasimeno. Its *castello* was refortified in 1297.

Then, as relative peace came to the region, the town built itself a superb church, the Madonna dei Miracoli. It dates from 1494 and is one of the finest renaissance monuments in the whole of Umbria. A master from Settignano named Domenico Bertini gave this church a splendid doorway in 1512, and the building is crammed with lovely seventeenth-century frescoes and paintings.

The unrivalled situation of a hilltown dominating a lake must often have proved irresistibly attractive in those more settled times when fortresses were being transformed into palaces. Today the mixture of architectural styles adds to their charm. Nemi in the Latium, for example, boasts a belvedere near its grey-walled *palazzo* from which you can gaze left up to the simple classical lines of the church of the Assumption. The pink stone of the church, its square clock tower and its silver, domed belfry rise above houses shuttered green and brown, some of them three or four storeys high. Look

RIGHT
Via Palazzaccio, Castel Rigone, with varied windows suggesting a complex architectural history.

LEFT
Olive groves and poppies flourish on the shores of Lake Nemi.

right and you are presented with a sheer drop of 200 metres to the green waters of Lake Nemi, whose every border is terraced and cultivated. Across the lake you can see the huddled roofs of Genzano, another hilltown (see p. 149). Aeneas Sylva rightly dubbed this redolent beauty spot the 'home of muses and nymphs'.

Nemi derives its name from a sacred grove (*nemus*) dedicated in Roman times to the goddess Diana. Drive through the massive arch of the *palazzo* and through another arch in the old town wall (whose ancient buttresses are held together by great metal clamps), and you can wind down Via del Tempio di Diana for 3 kilometres to the lake. The road is narrow, with the occasional passing place, trees rising on your right, trellised vines and olives sloping down on your left, with poppies forming splashes of red among the greens and browns. At the bottom of the hill, a T-junction offers you the choice of turning left to the museum of Roman ships or right to the remains of the temple of Diana. The museum used to house a couple of perfectly preserved vessels, built in the reign of Caligula (AD 37–41) and recovered from the lake around 1930. Both perished in flames in 1944, and the ships you see today are reproductions.

In these cities and towns you can thus walk directly from the Middle Ages (or even, in the case of Nemi, from antiquity) into the post Renaissance era, from walled towns whose warrens of narrow winding streets are often defended by a *rocca*, into a newer quarter where the architecture and monuments reflect the breath of humanism. Henry James's description of Montepulciano in Tuscany as 'brown and queer and crooked, and noble withal', could describe them all. In the neighbourhood he sensed that there was what he called 'a rumour of Etruscan towns'; certainly the name of the mountain on whose slopes the city stands, Monte di Totona, is Etruscan, and the Etruscan king Lars Porsena is traditionally regarded as the founder of Montepulciano.

Today its architectural monuments date back as far as the Middle Ages, as does the twisting pattern of its streets. In the Piazza Grande adjoining the cathedral is the late fourteenth-century Palazzo Comunale, battlemented as any fortress-palace ought to be and with a façade by the Florentine Michelozzo di Bartolommeo. It serves as the civic museum, well worth visiting to admire the della Robbia terracottas. Even better value is to climb the steps of the tower, the view from the top across the olive and cypress-studded landscape of Tuscany extending for some 65 kilometres as far as Siena and even to Lake Trasimeno in Umbria.

But such remnants of fortress Montepulciano are combined with renaissance urbanity. In front of the fourteenth-century Palazzo del Pretura is a well, guarded by two pedimented classical pillars crowned with a couple of lions and two griffons. The crumbling coat of arms sculpted on the well is that of the Medici. Flanking the square are two elegant palaces designed by Antonio da Sangallo the Elder in the first half of the sixteenth century, and another of his buildings, the Palazzo Cervini, can be seen in Via di Voltaia nel Corso. His flamboyance in refurbishing the medieval walls and the main gateway into Montepulciano in 1511 made him the darling of every rich family that wanted a new home in the fashionable style of the era.

Vignola too has been busy here, contributing the Palazzo Gagnoni-Grugni, in the same street as Palazzo Cervini, and Palazzo Tarugi and Palazzo Avignonesi, both in Via di Gracciano, the latter decorated with a couple of fairly mild lions' heads. Do these represent the lion of Florence, who appears proudly on a pillar close by just inside the city gate?

The cathedral itself was begun in 1592 and more or less finished by 1630 (save for work that still awaits completion). Given its present form by Ammanati and Ippolito Scalza, the influence of these two architects ensures that the building irrevocably says good-bye to the Middle Ages. Only its campanile, which also remains unfinished, derives from the earlier church that stood on this spot. Inside the cathedral Taddeo di Bartolo's 1401 triptych of the *Assumption of the Madonna*, showing Mary surrounded by angels and saints, gleams with gilt and rich colour. Michelozzo contributed to this cathedral a work of art that marks a turning point in the Renaissance assimilation of antiquity. In 1427 the Florentine humanist Bartolommeo Aragazzi, a courtier of the

This fifteenth-century Madonna was painted for the cathedral of Montepulciano by the Sienese master Sano di Pietro.

great Cosimo de' Medici, commissioned the artist to begin work on his tomb. Aragazzï died four years later, and in the *duomo* of Montepulciano he is commemorated by what, because of its spiritual and intellectual sources, is essentially the first humanist monument in Tuscany. Michelozzo has sculpted a blend of the valedictory sorrow exuded by pagan memorials and the sensual charm of his renaissance master Donatello.

Aragazzi was not the only notable humanist bred in Montepulciano. One of the most influential was Angelo Ambrogini, friend of Botticelli, the tutor of Lorenzo de' Medici (the poet and Platonist who ruled Florence in the second half of the fifteenth century) and his children. A plaque in Via dell'Opio marks the house where he was born. Out of love for his birthplace he took its Latin name, Mons Politianus, and called himself Politian (or in truth Poliziano). His own verse seems to laud that spring which was the Renaissance and that was even then transforming Montepulciano along with so many other Italian cities:

> *Ben venga maggio*
> *e 'l gonfalon selvaggio:*
> *Ben venga primavera*
> *che vuol l'uom s'innamori.*
> *E voi, donzelle, a schiera*
> *con li vostri amadori,*
> *che di rose e di fiori*
> *vi fate belle il maggio,*
> *venite alla frescura*
> *delli verdi arbuscelli.*
> *Ogni bella è sicura*
> *fra tanti damigelli;*
> *chè le fiere e gli uccelli*
> *ardon d'amore il maggio.*

Welcome, May, with your wild banner:
Welcome spring, which longs for men to fall in love.
And you crowd of maidens with your lovers,
making yourselves beautiful in May with roses and other flowers,
come to the freshness of the green bushes.
Each fair one is safe among so many young men;
because the beasts and the birds are ardent with love in May.

Autumn in Tuscany.

The renaissance masterpieces of Montepulciano are harmoniously juxtaposed with vestiges of the Middle Ages. In Via Ricci stands the gothic Palazzo Neri-Orselli, a museum with more della Robbia terracottas and a collection of Florentine and Sienese art that is as choice as it is small. The frescoed fourteenth-century Santa Maria dei Servi survives, as does another fourteenth-century church, Sant'Agnese, which stands just outside the Porta al Prato. Here too are frescoes, depicting the life of Montepulciano's patron saint, St Agnes. Her mortal remains lie here in an urn. Her shade emerges to

bless a country fair held annually in Montepulciano on 1 May, her feast day. But the transformation brought about in the town in the sixteenth century and after is evident even outside the walls. A brief walk away is the honey-coloured church of the Madonna di San Biagio, an early sixteenth-century treat whose tower is embellished with all four orders of architecture. Inspired by Bramante's design for St Peter's, Rome, Antonio da Sangallo the Elder built it in the form of a Greek cross to house a marble reredos which Gianozzo and Lisandro Albertini had designed in 1584. Apart from Santa Maria della Consolazione outside Todi, I know of no intimate renaissance church to match it. And I should like to be parish priest of San Biagio, for its rectory was also built by Sangallo and boasts a beautiful double loggia.

Yet in terms of ecclesiastical architecture, in spite of the contribution of Sangallo, this is Michelozzo's town, his genius at its busiest in the flowing classical façade of Sant'Agostino, set off by gothic buildings on either side. Artists of the calibre of Lorenzo di Credi and Giovanni d'Agostino contributed paintings to the church, but the wooden crucifix, carved in the fifteenth century, came from an earlier building. Opposite its façade rises the Torre di Pulcinella, a clock tower named after the comically incongruous manikin who strikes the hours.

The citizens of Montepulciano devote the last week of August to drinking their celebrated red wine. Because, some say, it was first fermented for use at Holy Communion, or because, as others say, it was initially drunk only by the aristocracy, the wine is dubbed *vino nobile*. A dissipated Henry James confessed that at Montepulciano he 'quaffed it too constantly'. This annual *baccanale* also involves eating a stomach-expanding dumpling or two (*panzatella*).

Those who enjoy pondering how cramped medieval townships can suddenly blossom into full-blown renaissance cities can derive a thrill similar to that offered by Montepulciano by visiting some of the Castelli Romani, the villages perched on rocky eminences around Rome which have served since ancient times as oases of fresh air during the dusty, breathless summers in the city itself. Montecompatri is set 576 metres above sea-level on a spur of volcanic tufa. Olive groves, woods, vineyards and forests give its surroundings the look of crumpled velvet and an air of effortless sumptuousness. Yet save for the occasional unsung hermit, no-one lived here until Tuscolo was razed. Then the Romans gave the spot its name, Mons Compitum, which roughly translated means hilly crossroad. Though at first sight Montecompatri looks like a purely medieval village, this spot is dominated by an elegant seventeenth-century church which is referred to as a cathedral. The late nineteenth-century restoration of this building was both necessary and occasionally clumsy.

Outside the village is a massive convent, dedicated to St Sylvester and built in 1603 on the spot where Pope Sylvester I is said to have given solace to Christians persecuted by the Romans in the early fourth century. In this building, too, the seventeenth century has conferred its own style on the lineaments of ancient Christianity, elegance supplanting austerity.

Not far away, Genzano di Roma clings fan-like to the south-west slopes of a hill, as if desperate to avoid sinking in the lake of Nemi. The lake itself was long reputed sacred

Looking down on San Biagio, Montepulciano, from Piazza San Francesco.

to the goddess Diana, or Cynthia, hence the derivation of Genzano from the ancient Cynthanium. Cistercian monks from the abbey of Tre Fontane were granted possession of the territory in 1183 by Pope Lucius III. Fifty years later they had constructed a fortified castle here. Medieval churchmen seem to have developed the habit of giving away territory more than once, and in 1378 Genzano was presented to the Orsini family by the anti-Pope Clement VII. Successive great families took over the castle, which in the mid sixteenth century finally passed into the hands of the Cesarini.

The seventeenth-century Palazzo Sforza Cesarino which they built in place of the fortress is far from elegant now and must surely one day be restored. It requires some imagination to spot that one is contemplating a once beautiful brick-and-stone, three-storey renaissance mansion. The sum of sprawling Genzano di Roma is at present less than its parts. Yet its festival of flowers, held annually for the past 200 years on the Sunday after the feast of Corpus Christi, must bring in enough money to fund a comprehensive restoration. Genzano's most elegant street, which rises to the cathedral, is entirely carpeted with flowers for this festival, laid out in patterns which feebly reflect the work of present-day, avant-garde artists.

Three kilometres away along the Via Appia Nova which leads to Rome stands the ancient Latin city of Ariccia. The viaduct paid for by the pope in 1843 obscures the fact that this town rises on a defensive height. Here Gian Lorenzo Bernini built the church of Santa Maria Assunta in Cielo in 1662. The master has somehow contrived to make the interior of his church airy and light, a perfectly circular place for rational worship, under a cupola which pushes up to a renaissance heaven. Swags and cherubs delight and comfort the faithful, and over the high altar a couple of angels, frescoed by Guglielmo Borgognone, are about to crown a modestly radiant Blessed Virgin.

Bernini was also responsible for the Piazza della Repubblica in front of the church, with its two handsome fountains. To explore the medieval and earlier origins of the town which he transformed, you must find Piazza Agostino Chigi, whose renaissance loggias scarcely prepare you for the view of the natural amphitheatre, a scooped-out crater, from which Ariccia rises. To the left you can see the medieval battlements of the turreted Porta Romana. If you need further proof that the seventeenth century has overwhelmed the glories of Latin and medieval Ariccia, venture outside the town to see the church of Santa Maria di Galloro, which boasts an utterly self-confident baroque façade, again by Bernini.

A recurrently pleasing feature of hilltowns is that whatever regrettable twentieth-century ugliness has been built around them, their constricted sites usually make it impossible for anyone to wreck the historic core. We shall see this at Cascia and the same phenomenon re-appears at Marino in Latium. The nastiness outside the old town disappears as you climb to reach suddenly narrowing cobbled streets, tall houses, churches and the sixteenth-century Palazzo Colonna – now the town hall. This palace appositely indicates that our forefathers displayed infinitely greater skill in adding to or transforming their towns and cities than we do. The Colonna family built it in place of the medieval castle after they had seized Marino from the Orsini family in 1419. As you walk around the palace, whose charm derives I think from the renaissance details –

RIGHT
This classical fountain in Genzano di Roma commemorates Pope Clement XIV, who died in 1774.

LEFT
Shutters lazily open onto Piazza Santa Barbara, Marino.

151

rounded stone arches, classical motifs over the windows – rather than from any
overbearing grandeur, you see that it still nestles against medieval battlements.

Climbing further you reach two churches, both of which express the classical dignity
of the seventeenth century. The first is the collegiate church of San Barnaba, graced by
a statue of St Barnabas by Giovanni Francesco Baribieri, who was known as Il Guercino.
Here too hangs a shield taken from the Turks at the battle of Lepanto in 1571, for the
admiral of the papal fleet was Marcantania Colonna of Marino. On the way to the second
you pass Marino's statue of the Moors in Piazza Matteotti, erected in exultation at this
same Christian victory. The poor Moors are chained, the women bare-breasted, the
negroid features of the men downcast and defeated. Close by the cruel renaissance
beauty of this fountain two stark medieval towers, one machicolated, poke into the sky,
a reminder of Marino's warlike past.

When you reach it, half-way up Corso Vittoria Colonna, the church of Santissima Trinità is equally satisfying inside and out. Beyond is the summit of the town, with marvellous views over the Albano lake and as far as Castelgandolfo and Monte Cavo. Woodlands are interspersed with vineyards, a reminder that Marino hosts a grape festival, usually in the first week of October, when the latest vintage of its wine, a paler gold than that of Frascati, flows from the fountain of the Moors.

As all these places reveal, the nature of the site determined architectural development in the past as much as it does today. Città della Pieve is a perfect example of this. Situated in Umbria on a ridge above the lower Chianti valley, the town prospered and developed in the Middle Ages, gradually spreading out around its twelfth-century *duomo*, one of whose two campaniles still betrays its romanesque beginnings. When it grew rich again in the sixteenth and seventeenth centuries, all the citizens were able to do was rebuild and restore what they had inherited from the past. There was no space for expansion.

This period of renewal saw the rebuilding of most of the cathedral, which was faced with marble. In the early sixteenth century the town's most celebrated son, Perugino, was employed to embellish its interior with superb paintings (a *Baptism of Jesus*, and a *Madonna with Saints*). In 1781 Città della Pieve gave its cathedral a second campanile, this one in the classical style. The medieval *rocca* still retains three of its towers, but the ambience of Città della Pieve derives nowadays much more from the Palazzo Bandini built by Galeazzo Alessi in the sixteenth century and from the near-contemporary Palazzo della Corcogna.

Jesi in the Marches, like Marino in Latium and Ariccia just outside Rome, offers both gastronomical and architectural pleasure. Scarcely 20 kilometres from the sea, set on the left bank of the River Esino, it has given its name to Verdicchio dei Castelli di Jesi, the wine made from grapes grown on the slopes below the often fortified villages which surround the picturesque town itself.

On Boxing Day 1194, Jesi was the birthplace of Frederick II Hohenstaufen. This was an unplanned event. His mother, Constanza of Sicily, was on her way to join her husband at Palermo when contractions suddenly began and the future Holy Roman Emperor was unexpectedly born in the shade of a market stall. In his adult years Frederick never forgot the town where he first saw the light of day. An inscription on the town hall records that as Holy Roman Emperor he confirmed all its privileges. Fourteenth-century walls still surround the medieval city, machicolated, punctuated with towers, and irregular in shape to match the contours of the hill. All the charm of a medieval hilltown is crammed into its narrow streets. Medieval Jesi has also preserved – just outside the ancient town – its romanesque church of San Marco, whose apse was frescoed in the fourteenth century. Here, too, you see the first hint of the Renaissance, in the classical tomb of the Nolfi family inside the church and in the composure of the eighteenth-century Clementine archway nearby.

And it is the baroque which dominates the Piazzale Centrale (or Piazza Federico II). This piazza stands on the site of the former Roman forum, and the cathedral which shades it is dedicated to a Roman Christian, St Septimius, first bishop of the city, who

155

RIGHT
A renaissance doorway at Jesi.

LEFT
A lion demonstrates his strength over the doorway of the Palazzo della Signoria, Jesi.

RIGHT
A renaissance doorway at Jesi.

RIGHT
These noble steps beckon worshippers into the church of San Pietro Apostolo in Jesi's Piazza Franciolini.

met his death by martyrdom in 308. Today, though its façade dates only from 1889, this is a gracious eighteenth-century building standing in an equally gracious eighteenth-century square, with the baroque Palazzo Balleani pointing up the classicism of the façades of a second, adjoining piazza. In the neighbouring square to the south stands the Palazzo della Signoria, the fifteenth-century home of the prominent Malatesta family (and after them the Sforzas). It was designed in 1486 by Francesco di Giorgio Martini, who, though Sienese, had assimilated the innovations of the Florentine Renaissance. As finished in 1498, this palace had a certain grim severity, but at the beginning of the sixteenth century Sansovino softened the original with a gracious courtyard and loggias. A doorway, decorated with the lion of the city's coat of arms, was added in 1588, thus further refining the whole ensemble. Today the Palazzo della Signoria is Jesi's municipal museum, exhibiting treasures covering the history of this city, from Roman remains through renaissance statuary to eighteenth-century ceramics.

A more arresting collection is housed in the elegant eighteenth-century Palazzo Pianetti-Tesei, now the civic gallery. Built in 1730, Palazzo Pianetti-Tesei includes a beautifully stuccoed rococo gallery, and other rooms decorated by the fanciful brush of P. Lazzarini. Many local artists are represented in the gallery, but their works are overshadowed by the paintings of the early sixteenth-century Venetian Lorenzo Lotto. Most notable is his *Deposition* of 1512, whose muted colours surely derive some of their charm from the influence of Raphael (whom Lotto had met in Rome in 1509 three years before he painted it.). Here too is an altarpiece depicting the troubles of St Lucy, painted by the mature artist in 1532.

Not far away stands the eighteenth-century theatre named after the composer Giovanni Battista Pergolesi, the city's favourite son, who died of tuberculosis in 1736 aged only twenty-six. He spent most of his short life in or near Naples, and is best known for his haunting *Stabat Mater*, composed in the year of his death.

Something about Jesi, with its steep tortuous streets, reminds me of Ragusa in Sicily. Whereas most hilltowns owe their appearance to man alone, Ragusa, like many a Sicilian city, suffers from earthquakes, and a particularly massive one of 1693 made necessary the construction of a complete new town. If Urbino was transformed by the will of a renaissance duke and Montepulciano by the influence of the Medici and the Florentine Renaissance, a goodly part of Ragusa developed from a medieval fortress into an elegant eighteenth-century city because of this natural disaster.

Ragusa is spectacularly situated on a ridge connecting two hills with deep gorges on either side. The city is in two distinct parts, a long flight of 242 steps linking modern Ragusa with the old town, Ragusa Ibla, which stands 113 metres below it. Whereas upper Ragusa was rebuilt in an orderly fashion, streets crossing each other at right-angles, Ragusa Ibla is infinitely more picturesque and untidy, not to say uneven and undulating. In the heaped-up confusion of its streets I remain continually astonished to come across superb buildings from the age of reason, yet at the foot of the steps three of them instantly appear: the baroque palazzi Bertini and Cosentini, and the church of Santa Maria dell'Idria.

The lower town also has one of Ragusa's two eighteenth-century cathedrals.

Ragusa Ibla rises in the distance, viewed across one of the two ravines which isolate the city.

159

Designed by Rosario Gagliardi in 1738, the cathedral of San Giorgio was not finished till 1775 and its classical dome was added only in 1820. San Giorgio is like few other cathedrals of this period. A staircase flanked by wrought-iron railings rises to its undulating façade, a sinuous composition adorned with swags, columns, frills, stone torches, pediments, statues and an ornamental balcony. The cathedral in the upper town is much more severe, its massive classical façade broken with Corinthian columns.

The two Ragusas entrancingly blend the baroque with the gothic. Piazza Pola is overlooked by the baroque Palazzo Donnafugato and the baroque façade of the late sixteenth-century church of San Giuseppe. Its altars are richly decorated, and its patron saint (St Joseph) is represented in a seventeenth-century statue by a master silversmith named Filippo Paladino. Nearby, the porch of the church of San Antonio is an example of the ornate Sicilian gothic, and a more restrained gothic is found in the doorway of San

160

Giorgio Vecchio, on whose tympanum St George spiritedly kills the dragon.

Tuscany and Latium draw this chapter to a conclusion. If its two canyons add a spine-tingling thrill to Ragusa, Pitigliano, 74 kilometres south of Grosseto, is set on a rocky escarpment that overlooks no fewer than three deep ravines. The Etruscans settled here, burying their dead in caverns in the volcanic rock and defending their tombs with a massive wall, part of which still stands on either side of the Porta Capo di Sotto. In more modern times, Pitigliano became supremely important in the late thirteenth century when the Orsini family made it one of their principal seats, building the formidable castle which was to be transformed into an elegant *palazzo* in the fifteenth and sixteenth centuries, when much of the rest of the town was rebuilt. You can experience a sense of the transition from medieval village to palatial renaissance city simply by walking across Pitigliano's slender Piazza della Repubblica, which pokes its long finger between them. But although part of the medieval town has lasted intact into our own century, its chief adornments are the renaissance church of Santa Maria and the baroque cathedral. The medieval ghetto, inhabited by the Jewish community which established itself here in the fifteenth century ought also to have survived, but the Jews were exterminated by the fascists in World War II. All that persists of their scholarship and civilization are remnants of a synagogue in Vicolo Manin.

But perhaps the most impressive of these renaissance hilltowns is Frascati, one of the Castelli Romani. Here above all the wealthy Romans used to escape their hot capital, building luxurious villas for themselves, for the *savants* whom they cultivated and who in turn sang their praises, and languishing with their families and friends – writers, politicians, lawyers – throughout the oppressive summer. Here lived Cicero, the man described by Catullus as the worst of all poets and the finest of all orators:

> *tanto pessimus omnium poeta,*
> *quanto tu optimus omnium patronus.*

Modern Frascati, however, is famous not for its Roman remains but for its sixteenth- and seventeenth-century villas, built here for the courtiers, cardinals, princes and artists who surrounded the papal court after the sixteenth-century Pope Paul III made the town his favoured summer retreat. The most impressive, overlooking Piazza Giacomo Marconi, is the classical Villa Aldobrandini, the most articulately civilized of all the renaissance buildings of this exceedingly urbane city. Terraced green lawns roll up to the perfectly regular yet never boring façade, with its pedimented central bay and two low wings. Rows of windows tickle one's sensibilities quite insensibly (to use one of Gibbon's favourite words), their shapes cunningly varied, sometimes square, sometimes twice as high as they are broad, with the three at the apex of the villa slightly arched. Although I have visited Frascati several times, I never feel I have succeeded in finding the key to the attractiveness of this building.

Villa Aldobrandini shares the name of Cardinal Pietro Aldobrandini, who was given the house by his uncle Pope Clement VIII in 1598. Pietro decided that his uncle's gift deserved extending, and commissioned Giacomo della Porta to remodel it. Giacomo persuaded the cardinal that nothing short of a complete transformation was required.

Elegant Frascati, a city of classical renaissance palaces.

Though Giacomo died in 1602, his plans were executed, and his successor Carlo Maderno finally completed the work in 1604. Maderno also realized the spectacular water theatre, devised by the ingenious Giacomo on the steep slope behind the villa, with its water effects and statues of mythological figures. Jets spurt out in front of the statues, dramatic cascades plunge down the hill, and paths lead upwards through woods of oaks and chesnuts above.

Frascati still preserves some steep, narrow streets, but these open into broad *piazze*, such as the Piazza San Pietro, with its glamorous renaissance fountain, and a church inscribed with the date MDCC. This building turns out to be the cathedral. The date in fact refers only to the completion of the elaborately classical façade, designed by Girolamo Fontana in 1697, its lower columns Doric, the upper ones Ionic. As the inscription half-way up proclaims, the reigning pope was Clement XI. Bernardino Cometti carved the relief over the central doorway, depicting Jesus reproving poor St Peter for his lack of faith.

Frascati cathedral is strangely bare inside, in spite of the grandiose pillars which separate its three naves and the nineteenth-century frescoes in its Chapel of the Blessed Sacrament. The very existence of its cupola surprises you, since not a trace of it can be seen from the outside. Its architect Girolamo Fontana is honoured in a memorial on the west wall to the right of the entrance. If you search diligently enough, you will find a fourteenth-century icon in the Chapel of the Redeemer, as well as a couple of sixteenth-century statues representing Saints Agatha and Lucy.

Once as I explored this cathedral I was approached by two ladies who – in a southern Irish accent poignantly reminiscent of my long-dead Granny Daley – asked me in Italian to point them to the memorial to the Catholic Stuart. I took them to the left of the entrance, where a plaque commemorates Charles Edward, the Young Pretender, whose father (the Old Pretender) laid claim to the throne of England, Scotland, France and Ireland as James VI. Here too is buried Charles Edward's son Henry Benedict, the coat of arms of Great Britain above his memorial, though why he should have been concerned with his dubious British inheritance when he became a Cardinal of the Roman Catholic church and Bishop of Tusculum, I cannot imagine.

Frascati welcomes the curious traveller. I shall never forget in the mid 1980s walking into the eighteenth-century Chiesa del Gesù (consecrated by Henry Benedict Stuart in 1733), remembering from a previous visit Andrea Pozzo's *trompe l'oeil* baldacchino inside and longing to relish it a second time. As you enter the church and walk towards the baldacchino, your eyes accustoming themselves to the gloom, it appears to move ahead of you, as does the fake painted cupola above it. The verger was sweeping the floor, and as I was the only visitor he kindly stopped and began talking to me. He showed me the place, in the middle of the church just before the crossing, where Antarto Colli's *trompe l'œil* cupola appears absolutely regular and perfect. Then I realized that we were not speaking in Italian but in English, and that this courteous verger had the broad vowels of a Yorkshire accent. He told me that, as a soldier in World War II, he had been captured in 1941, been a prisoner of war in Egypt and India, and then spent his last eight months of captivity in Sheffield and Hull.

# 5

# PILGRIMS AND
# SHRINES

F ACED WITH THE INEVITABILITY of death, and constantly reminded of their mortality by plagues, sickness and war, men and women since antiquity have turned to religion to mitigate its threat. They did so first of all by pouring their wealth into churches built to the glory of God and in the hope of salvation. A second popular technique for pursuing the road to heaven was the pilgrimage. The three Meccas of Christian pilgrims were Jerusalem, where Jesus was crucified, Rome, where the apostles Peter and Paul were martyred, and later Santiago de Compostela in northern Spain, where the bones of St James the Great were enshrined. Here heaven seemed to reach down to earth. Each pilgrim saw the journey to these shrines as a model of the course of human life. Each was performing a personal drama of the human condition in the quest for salvation. Each remembered the example of the patriarch Abraham, commanded by God to leave his own country to seek the promised land.

In addition to the three great shrines of Christendom, a number of other places had acquired sacred associations, especially those where the bones of a holy man or woman or some other physical symbol of the divine could be found. Europe was crammed with them. To quote the historian Christopher Brooke, 'The spiritual treasury of medieval Europe was inexhaustible. Every church had its relics; most great churches had the shrine of a local saint who attracted pilgrims from his own country.'

A pilgrimage was also a most enjoyable affair, usually made in the company of like-minded men and women who were occupied not just with piety but also with games, story-telling and the pursuit of new experiences. We know that pilgrims relished the sights and tastes of travel. Very early on in Christian history the pilgrimage routes even produced a number of travel writers, who wrote guides for those who might come after them. The first such account to have survived, the *Itinerarium burdigalense*, was written as early as the year 333 by a pilgrim from Bordeaux. The next, the *Peregrinatio* of Etheria, written around 400, describes the journey of a Spanish noblewoman to the Holy Land. Both contain fascinating topographical detail. Later medieval pilgrimage guides would even offer advice on food and drink and where to stay.

Among the many famed pilgrimage centres of Italy was the hilltown of Orvieto. I believe the medieval pilgrim must have thrilled quite as much as the modern traveller to the spectacular approach on the road from Viterbo. Today, pine trees, spruce and acacia shade the way, which winds through vineyards interspersed with the roses so assiduously cultivated by the people of this region. Then the city suddenly appears across the valley of the River Paglia, set high up on a 325-metre crag of red volcanic rock, its roofs and towers dominated by the mass of the cathedral. What the pilgrim later discovered to be the belfry and church of San Francesco, the papal palace, the Torre del Moro and the Palazzo del Capitano del Popolo glint pink in the sunlight. The tortuous road spins down and then snakes up again to reach the city walls.

Yet the pilgrim's inspiration was never primarily that of the tourist, but of the religious, hungry and thirsty for the divine. Orvieto's attraction for Christian pilgrims (who still flock here) derived not from its extraordinary beauty, but from what to many people today must seem an abstruse metaphysical debate and a scarcely credible miracle. The key to understanding what happened in Orvieto is the odd, if beautiful, church of San Domenico. On its façade, golden brown tufa sets off grey and white striped square pillars, some still only partly faced. The interior is even odder, for the church turns out to be four times as broad as it is long. On the left of the entrance is Arnolfo di Cambio's monument of 1282 to Cardinal de Braye, one of those Frenchmen brought in to run the city by Pope Martin IV.

San Domenico's greatest treasure is even stranger. Displayed in a showcase to the left of the altar is a simple medieval chair. From this humble seat, the great medieval theologian St Thomas Aquinas taught and preached in thirteenth-century Orvieto. The time was ripe for Aquinas's most celebrated contribution to Christian theology. By good fortune in 1263 he was living at the Dominican monastery that once adjoined this church when the miracle occurred which made Orvieto one of the greatest pilgrimage centres of western Christendom. The miracle also provoked the building of its superb cathedral.

At this moment the greatest brains of western Christendom, as well as the humblest priests and the thinking laity, were preoccupied with one question: how did the bread and wine used at the Christian Mass become for believers the body and blood and Jesus? According to one of Aquinas's biographers, his own devotion to the sacrament of Holy Communion was extraordinary. 'He spent several hours of the day, and part of the night, before the altar, humbling himself in acts of profound adoration and melting with love in contemplation of the Man-God, whom he there adored. In saying mass he seemed to be in raptures, and often quite dissolved in tears; a glowing frequently appeared in his eyes and countenance, which showed the ardour with which his heart burnt within him.'

In this highly charged atmosphere a priest from Bohemia, Peter of Prague, doubting that bread and wine could ever convey Christ's body and blood to believers, journeyed to St Peter's, Rome, and on the tomb of St Peter himself begged for the gift of faith. He set off back to Prague, staying on the way at Bolsena just outside Orvieto. While he was celebrating mass there in the crypt of the church of Santa Cristina, the longed-for miracle occurred. As Peter of Prague raised aloft a piece of bread which he had just consecrated, blood poured out of it, staining the piece of linen (the corporal) placed under the chalice on the altar. This blood, it seemed, could only be that of Jesus himself. A divine sign had proved the truth of the doctrine of transubstantiation.

Pope Urban IV ordered that this corporal, still stained with the blood of Jesus,

The western aspect of Orvieto.

should be brought to Orvieto. On his orders Aquinas composed a remarkable hymn, *Pange lingua, gloriosi Corporis mysterium*, celebrating the miracle of transubstantiation:

> Word made Flesh, by word he makes
> Very bread his Flesh to be;
> Man in wine Christ's Blood partakes;
> And if senses fail to see,
> Faith alone the true heart wakes
> To behold the mystery.

From this seat in San Domenico, Aquinas urged his fellow Christians to worship the real presence of Jesus's body and blood in the bread and wine of the mass:

> Therefore we, before him bending,
> This great Sacrament revere;
> Types and shadows have their ending,
> For the newer rite is here;
> Faith, our outward sense befriending,
> Makes the inward vision clear.

Beside themselves with religious ecstasy, the Orvietans responded magnificently. Surely a new church, greater than any they had yet built, must house the corporal. Two ancient churches in the centre of their city were speedily demolished. On 13 November 1290 Urban IV's successor, Pope Nicholas IV, laid the first stone of their new and as it turned out stupendous cathedral.

It is a short step from San Domenico in Piazza XXIX Marzio to this cathedral. Its west façade is rightly acclaimed as among the supreme masterpieces of Italian gothic. Blue and pink, gold and green, decked with mosaics, twisting columns and a powerful rose window, the whole is in exuberant contrast to the calm elegance of the green and white stripes which decorate the romanesque apse and side walls. Arnolfo di Cambio probably created the first design, and the Perugian monk and architect Fra Bevignato began building the cathedral in 1290. His successor, a local architect named Giovanni Uguccione, was so inept that soon the new cathedral was in danger of collapsing. The Orvietans turned to a genius, the Sienese architect and sculptor Lorenzo Maitani. To Maitani Orvieto cathedral owes its celebrated façade and the majority of the remarkable reliefs that embellish it.

The basic structure of the façade is conventional enough, with four polygonal towers framing three sections which reflect the nave and aisles inside. For the cornice which runs above the doorways, Maitani sculpted in bronze the symbols of the four evangelists; Matthew, Mark, Luke and John. For the lintel of the main doorway he designed a canopy held aloft by angels to shelter a Madonna and Child carved by Andrea Pisano in 1347. Between 1354 and 1380 Orcagna created the rose window above, placing at its centre a carving of the head of Jesus.

Finer even than these works of religious art are the exquisite bas-reliefs carved at the

Sculpted by Maitani, the winged bull, symbol of St Luke, peers cheekily from the façade of the cathedral at Orvieto.

foot of the four towers. Once again they are the work of Maitani. Running from left to right they illustrate the biblical tales of creation and the fall of mankind. The dove-like spirit of God broods over chaos, out of which God creates both Eve and Adam, the former from one of Adam's ribs. In spite of a heavenly warning, the two humans eat forbidden fruit, tempted by a serpent which coils around the tree on which the fruit grows. Driven from their earthly paradise, they are barred by an eternal fire which surrounds it. Their sons quarrel, and Cain murders Abel. So the saga continues into the next panel to recount God's response to human folly, ending with the angel announcing to the Virgin Mary that a divine child will be conceived in her womb. The next two series of carvings depicts his life. Jesus is crucified, rises from death and finally is depicted judging the world, the damned consigned to perdition, the saved to heavenly bliss. Sinuous branches of ivy, vine or acanthus frame each episode. The reliefs are busy

but never fussy, the techniques of the sculptors breathtakingly delicate. And the human folly with which the tale began is never far from their minds; on the far right the damned are depicted writhing in misery, one poor sinner clasping his hands to his ears as if to blot out the terrifying news.

The mosaics on the west façade, which date from the fourteenth to the nineteenth centuries, recount the life of the Virgin Mary to whom this cathedral is dedicated. Treasures inside also celebrate her, particularly the fourteenth-century frescoes in the apse and a superb fresco of the *Madonna and Child* by Gentile da Fabriano. He painted it in 1425, only two years before his death. The Virgin wears an agitated blue robe, lined with green. By looking closely you can see that Gentile even painted the red stitching. Next to it stands a splendidly animated font created by Luca di Giovanni sixty-five years later. Sano di Matteo added the gothic temple on top of which perches John the Baptist. A yet more exuberant piece adjoins the font, a holy water stoup designed by Ippolito Scalza. For this cathedral Scalza also carved (out of one block of marble) an astonishingly lively *Pietà*, given the supposed deadness of its subject. As for the apse, Maitani himself designed much of the stained glass in its slender east window, as well as supervising the construction of the elaborate choir-stalls made by Giovanni Ammanati of Siena in 1329.

The overall design of Orvieto cathedral, with its white and green bands of stone and rich capitals, exudes peace. On the west wall, beneath the icy blue tones of the rose window, is a delicately arched clerestory. The renaissance pulpit is worth pausing over, its elegant lines carved out of wood in 1622 by Marcanti, a native of the city. Even more remarkable are the frescoes of the so-called New Chapel, which is sometimes also known as the Chapel of San Brizio. Built at the end of the fourteenth century, it was initially partly frescoed by Fra Anglico and Benozzo Gozzoli. After their deaths, the chapter of Orvieto cathedral commissioned Luca Signorelli to finish the work. Signorelli's master was the sublime Piero della Francesca, whose genius we have already admired at Urbino (see pp. 127–37). Piero was an artist adept at contrasting naked or skin-clothed figures with graver, fully-clothed men and women. Signorelli's second master was the remarkable Florentine Antonio Pollaiuolo. From Pollaiuolo he learned above all how to exploit the way the muscles of men and women contort themselves under strain.

He began work on 5 April 1499. Fra Angelico and Benozzo Gozzoli had finished only two sections, one depicting Christ judging the world from the heavenly clouds, and a second showing prophets singing his glory. Even if this second scene were not readily recognizable from the inscription PROPHETARVM LAVDABILIS NVMERVS, there would be no problem distinguishing it from Signorelli's fresco of the doctors of the church (inscribed DOCTORVM SAPIENS ORDO), which was completed fifty years later. The richer colours of Signorelli's doctors, their individual postures and varied gestures add far more animation to his scene.

So impressed were the cathedral authorities that the following year they extended the commission, and Signorelli was asked to paint the walls of the entire chapel. For the whole fresco they offered Signorelli 575 ducats. He arranged for them to pay him partly

The richly decorated façade of Orvieto cathedral, with its thirteenth-century Byzantine mosaics, intricately carved west porticos and delicate balustrade.

in kind, providing him with a house with two beds, two monthly bushels of wheat and 125 litres of wine a year. Signorelli responded by producing a virtually unmatched renaissance masterpiece. Building on what he had learnt from Piero della Francesca, he frescoed a *Last Judgment* in which the naked damned and saved writhe in either torment or ecstasy, while stately clothed angels display their lordship over creation. As for the devils, they too are mostly naked, Pollaiuolo's pioneering depiction of straining human anatomy is brought to perfection in his pupil's inspired work.

There is, I think, more than a hint of sadism in the *Last Judgment*, especially in Signorelli's depiction of a devil flying away with a terrified woman on its back. To all this Signorelli added a waywardly fascinating panel devoted to stories of the anti-Christ. The panel includes a false Jesus, preaching not salvation but damnation (for behind him stands a horned devil, whispering wicked thoughts into his ear). Elsewhere in the panel an archangel flings the anti-Christ out of heaven. This was the scene in which the artist included his own self-portrait. He looks out at us, long hair falling below his hat. Behind he depicted a short-haired man wearing a skull-cap, his predecessor Fra Angelico. For some reason Luca Signorelli scorned any representation of Benozzo Gozzoli.

At the other side of the cathedral, in the left transept, is an ornate organ case designed by Ippolito Scalza and restored in 1975 (when its original 4000 pipes were augmented by 1585 more). In this same transept is the entrance to the Chapel of the Holy Corporal. You can see the corporal itself only twice yearly, on Easter Day and on the feast of Corpus Christi. Then the blood-soaked relic is carried to each quarter of the city. Three hundred Orvietans, colourfully dressed as medieval knights, magistrates, captains, standard-bearers and the nobility of yesteryear, parade in the procession.

When not on display the holy corporal is housed in a beautiful silver-gilt reliquary designed in the late 1330s by Ugolino di Vieri. What is more, he charmingly modelled its façade on the façade of the cathedral itself. Then he displayed another of his skills and added enamel panels recounting the miracle of the bleeding host. The chapel itself is worthy of the famous relic. Frescoes depicting the same miracle act as a foil for a huge marble tabernacle by the Florentine Andrea di Cione (who is better known as Orcagna). It is big enough to conceal most of a frescoed *Crucifixion*, so that all you can see are the dying thieves on either side of Jesus. Finally the Orvietans chose this chapel as the home of a painting by Lippo Memmi which depicts fortunate sinners taking refuge under the blue robe of a gentle Virgin Mary, who prays on their behalf.

This, then, is the superb masterpiece built to enshrine the visible relic of a medieval miracle. Inevitably the popes attempted to control a city so blessed. The citizens took the side of the popes in the struggle against the Holy Roman Emperor, yet jealously preserved their independence in the face of secular papal pretensions. The city remained a commune, governed from 1199 under a chief magistrate known as the *podestà*, the first of whom, Pietro Paranzo, was assassinated by supporters of the Emperor. Even the city's cherished autonomy from the papacy was continually at risk, and in the 1280s one pope managed for a time to replace the governors of Orvieto with Frenchmen loyal to himself. In 1364 Cardinal Albornoz, ever ready to promote the power of his papal masters, was commissioned by Innocent IV to build the fortress on the eastern side of the city whose ruins are now the public park.

An earlier architectural sign of papal power is the half-romanesque, half-gothic Palazzo del Capitano del Popolo. Pope Hadrian IV commissioned the earliest parts in 1157. Later the people of Orvieto added an ornate hall and the belfry at the east end. The delicate mullioned windows add entrancement. Why is a man's head cheekily grinning in one of them? A later papal gift is a remarkable artesian well, commissioned from Antonio Sangallo the Younger by Pope Clement VII after he had fled to Orvieto when Rome was sacked in 1527. Dedicated to St Patrick, it is almost 14 metres wide and 32 metres deep. What is more, you can walk down into it, using two concentric spiral staircases which neither meet nor cross each other. The only problem is that each staircase has 248 steps and the well grows colder and colder as you descend.

Orvieto grew rich on the pilgrims who flocked here and this wealth is reflected in a number of palaces and fine houses. The cathedral is surrounded by some of them. A colonnaded building to the south, now the cathedral museum, was once a papal palace, dating from the end of the thirteenth and the first half of the fourteenth centuries. Its treasures include a fragmentary fresco which carries yet another self-portrait of Luca Signorelli. Beyond this palace rises the Palazzo Buzi, which Ippolito Scalza built around 1580. And the cathedral square is dominated by the Torre di Maurizio, named after the man who in 1351 cast the bells which the tower carries, a name which has been usurped by the figure in the peaked hat who rings them.

The powerful Palazzo Faina, now an archaeological museum full of Etruscan treats (including a splendid Venus excavated from the nearby necropolis of Cannicella), is not far away, along the picturesquely narrow Via Maitani. Orvieto also houses a fine sprinkling of other lovely churches, among them the thirteenth-century San Francesco in Via Maitani, whose interior, surprisingly, turns out to be classical and whose brick and stone cloisters were designed by Ippolito Scalza, and the pale-brown church of San Lorenzo de Arari further to the south. Built between the thirteenth and fifteenth centuries, the latter includes a fresco depicting a busy St Lawrence saving souls, helping the lame, the sick and the poor, arraigned before a king and finally martyred on a griddle while an evil torturer fans the flames with a pair of bellows. Then there are the romanesque churches of San Rocco, with its sixteenth-century frescoes, and Sant'Andrea, in Piazza della Repubblica, whose twelve-sided and battlemented campanile has three rows of double-arched lights letting out the sound of its bells; over the centuries it has been embellished with ecclesiastical coats of arms carved out of stone.

Abutting onto Sant'Andrea is the symbol of the secular authority in Orvieto, the Palazzo Comunale, a thirteenth-century foundation transformed into a mid sixteenth-century palace by the vivacious Ippolito Scalza. Seven massive arches support its balcony, the middle one wide enough to drive a car through. And a perpetual reminder of the importance of Orvieto's twenty-four medieval guilds is the 42-metre-high Torre del Moro, for in 1316 they paid for its bell and embellished it with their coats of arms. It still chimes the hours.

If many a modern intellect finds the miracle of the bleeding host of Bolsena hard to accept, that which lies at the heart of Loreto is even more difficult to swallow. Lying in the Marches 24 kilometres south of Ancona, Loreto is famed for the shrine known as the Holy House of the Blessed Virgin Mary. It measures a mere ten by four metres. In the year 1472 a scholar named Pietro di Giorgio Tolomei recorded the tradition that this brick-built house once stood in Nazareth and had been the home of the mother of Jesus. Here, the story continues, the Angel Gabriel announced to Mary that she would bear the son of God. After Mary left this world, the tradition insists, Jesus's apostles transformed her home into a little church. St Luke, reputed to be the artist among the four Evangelists, sculpted a statue for this church, representing both Jesus's mother and her divine son.

In 1291 the Latin kingdom of Jerusalem, which had been established by the Crusaders in the Levant in 1099, fell to the heathen. Nazareth no longer seemed a fit or safe place for the former home of the Blessed Virgin Mary. On 10 May in that year angels therefore miraculously transported her house to Trsat, near Rijeka in Yugoslavia. The people of Trsat proved unworthy of the gift, insufficiently reverencing the Holy House. On 10 December 1294, the angels decided to move the home once more, this time to Recanati, which lies a mere 4 kilometres south-east of Loreto. Once again the response of the locals disappointed them, so on 2 December 1295 the Holy House was finally divinely transported to its present place of rest, a grove of laurels, the Latin for which, Lauretum, is the origin of the name Loreto.

The people of Loreto, unaware of the provenance of this little building, nonetheless were sufficiently responsive to its miraculous appearance to build a protective wall around it and from time to time to sweep out the house. A year after its arrival, the Blessed Virgin herself appeared to an old man in a dream, revealing the origin of the Holy House. The citizens were ready to be convinced. Nevertheless they took care to dispatch sixteen of their fellows to Nazareth, charged with measuring the foundations of the former home of Jesus's mother. There these emissaries discovered an inscription declaring that it had disappeared. They returned to Loreto convinced that the Holy House was genuine.

Soon many others shared the same conviction, including popes. To Boniface IX in 1320 the shrine clearly embodied the former home of Mary. In the 1470s, inspired no doubt by Pietro di Giorgio Tolomei of Teramo, Pope Paul II described the spot as 'founded by a miracle' and 'accompanied by angels'. Within a decade the shrine was granted special papal protection, and in 1507 a bull of Pope Julius II accepted at least that 'the pious believe' it was transported thither by angels. By now miracles were regularly occurring in connection with the Holy House.

Unlike Orvieto, which existed long before the miracle of the bleeding corporal, but like Monreale (see pp. 43–7), which established itself as a city around its great church, Loreto exists as a town simply because of the miraculous Holy House. The basilica which protects it, built between 1468 and 1587, rises powerfully above you as you drive up around the walls. A curious walkway circles its elegant apses, designed so that sentries might patrol the spot to defend the holy shrine.

Luigi Vanvitelli's mid eighteenth-century belfry beside the dome of Loreto's basilica.

The beautiful classical façade of the basilica, designed by Donato Bramante in 1571, rises above the Piazza della Madonna, with shallow steps leading up to three bronze doors cast between 1590 and 1610 which depict scenes from the Old and New Testaments. Beside the basilica, a campanile built in 1794 by Luigi Vanvitelli points some 90 or so metres into the skies. Among its bells is one weighing 11 tonnes, paid for by Pope Leo X in 1516. The left-hand side of the square is flanked by the sumptuous colonnaded Palazzo Apostolico, this too possibly by Bramante. It houses Loreto's art gallery, with fine works by Lorenzo Lotti and some Brussels tapestries based on Raphael cartoons. The centre of the piazza is adorned by a renaissance fountain, created by Carlo Maderno and Giovanni Fontana at the beginning of the seventeenth century and decorated with Pietro Paolo Iacometti's bronzes in 1622, its wide basin set on a shallow, stepped plinth.

177

The Holy House itself stands under the basilica's octagonal dome, designed by Giuliano da Sangallo in the style of Brunelleschi. In 1527, assisted by thirty fellow artists and craftsmen, Andrea Sansovino surrounded it with a marble shrine. Crowds press into the three aisles and chapels of the basilica. Ignoring the superb frescoes by Luca Signorelli in the sacristy of St John as well as those painted with remarkable luminosity in the sacristy of St Mark by Melozzo da Forli in 1477, their sole aim is a glimpse of and a prayer before (or even within) the Holy House. So many pilgrims were coming to Loreto by the early sixteenth century that the Medici Pope Clement VII made the drastic decision to close up the sole doorway of Mary's former home and create three others. This left a few bricks over, so the pope arranged for the height of the walls to be raised. His architects added a ceiling. The walls of the Holy House consist of oddly sized brown bricks, irregularly pieced together, an incongruously humble abode that contrasts with the marble altar and the rich golden lamps that hang on either side.

Amongst the statues of some of the fifty or so popes who have visited the Holy House is a chubby one of John XXIII, who came here in 1962, and a colossal one of Pope Sixtus V, who granted Loreto the status of a town in 1586. The cult of the Holy House and that of Our Lady of Loreto spread throughout Europe, as far away, for example, as northern France, where a replica of the basilica rises on a ridge in the Pas-de-Calais north of Arras, or to Bavaria, where visitors to the exquisite Franciscan nunnery of Kloster Reutberg discover that its full dedication is the Klosterkirche Maria Loreto auf dem Reutberg. Over the high altar of this church stands a reproduction of St Luke's statue of the Madonna. A Loreto cycle of prayers was decreed official for the whole of Italy in 1916. In 1920 Our Lady of Loreto was declared the patron saint of airmen.

Yet is this house, revered by countless pilgrims, really the Nazareth home of the Blessed Virgin? The devil's advocate in the historical controversy was a Frenchman, Ulysse Chevalier, whose book *Notre-Dame de Lorette: Étude historique sur l'authenticité de la Santa Casa* appeared in Paris in 1906. Chevalier vigorously argued that the first mention of the Virgin Mary's home at Nazareth occurs only in the year 1291. No-one in the Holy Land, he added, had referred to its disappearance before the sixteenth century. And until Pietro di Giorgio Tolomei published his speculations, few authorities even countenanced the idea that the Holy House had reached Loreto.

Against Chevalier, defenders of the tradition have argued that the type of bricks and mortar out of which the house is built are not local to the Marches, but they are common in Nazareth. These defenders also ask the pertinent question why a non-ecclesiastical building which clearly once was a three-roomed house should be found in a church unless it already possessed some holy connotation before arriving there. In addition, as they observe, the Holy House has no existing foundations, which implies that it must originally have stood somewhere else.

Even if this truly is the authentic former home of the Blessed Virgin Mary, the question whether angels transported it to Loreto by way of Yugoslavia and Recanati still has to be faced. On one visit to the shrine I managed to discuss this matter with one of the priests who usually hover in black robes around the altar inside the Holy House. He offered the interesting suggestion that in truth the Virgin Mary's home did not fly to

Loreto but was brought back, brick by brick, by pilgrims and crusaders returning from the Holy Land. He showed me a pamphlet which offers the information that in 1292 part of the dowry of a wife of the King of Naples included 'the holy stones of our Lady, Mother of God', carried from the Holy Land. He told me that some thirteenth-century coins as well as a medieval ostrich's egg have been found underneath the Holy House, indicating that the building probably did arrive here in the late Middle Ages.

Even as he offered me these weak buttresses of a virtually indefensible legend, I was aware that none of these problems crossed the minds of the faithful. Although it was an exceedingly rainy February afternoon, a good half of the Piazza della Madonna was crowded with pilgrims. Inside the basilica a massive congregation crammed itself into the seats and stood in the aisles. Men and women of all ages chanted the rosary led by one of my companion's fellow-priests. I retreated back into the piazza and to the comparative calm of the Hotel Santuario Ristorante.

Loreto is never empty, and on specially sacred days it fills to overflowing. On 10 December (the anniversary of the day the Holy House landed in Italy), bonfires light up the night throughout the countryside. What the faithful can never now see is the statue of the Virgin and Child allegedly carved by St Luke. In its day the statue suffered many vicissitudes. Taken to Paris in 1798, it was returned by Napoleon Bonaparte three years later. A fire consumed it in 1921, and all we see today is a replica, sculpted out of cedar wood and usually dressed in a magnificent bejewelled costume.

A more authentic medieval statue of the Mother of Jesus is the black virgin of Tindari in Sicily. Byzantine in origin, this miracle-working statue has turned black with the natural ageing of its wood and with centuries of smoke from flickering candles. Like many such black Virgins (for example, the celebrated images at Altötting in Bavaria and at Rocamadour in south-west France), that of Tindari has become yet more treasured by reason of its discoloration. Medieval Christians loved to recite the love poem in the Song of Songs which runs, 'I am black but comely', applying this celebration of physical beauty to the Mother of Jesus. In consequence, a statue which over the centuries blackened itself was deemed to have become more and more like the Virgin Mary herself. Small wonder such images provoked miracles in the lives of the faithful.

At Tindari the Black Virgin is enshrined in a huge, modern golden church, domed like that at Loreto and almost certainly standing on the site of the former acropolis of what was once a great Roman city. Sicilians make a point of annually walking up the hill to venerate the Madonna Nera on 8 September. Its piazza is rightly known as the Piazza Belvedere, for here you can ignore the stalls selling replicas of the Black Virgin and gaze at the magnificent view which stretches far across the Tyrrhenian Sea to the Aeolian islands. The cliff upon which Tindari stands seems to fall sheer into the waters. The town is also worth visiting for its Greek and Roman remains. From the shrine itself, Via Teatro Greco runs as far as the excavated sites, passing on the way vestiges of walls dating back to the Greek era which are still punctuated with towers and a double-arched gateway. A Greek theatre dating from the third century BC appears, modified by the Romans for their more brutal sports. Gladiators and wild animals once killed each other here. Today the theatre has the air of an old folks' garden by the sea, but then you notice the dank archway through which once emerged bloodthirsty beasts and yet more bloodthirsty human beings. Nearby are the remains of a late imperial basilica (for some reason known as the gymnasium) and the ancient baths, decorated with mosaics.

To my mind the spirituality of Byzantium emerges far more strongly in the monastery at Grottaferrata in Latium than in the Black Virgin of Tindari. Set 312 metres above sea-level, Grottaferrata today is mostly a modern town, its bustling main street offering the usual mini-markets and bars. Drive or walk along the one-way Corso del Popolo looking for signs to the Abbazio di San Nilo, which point you to a surprise: apparently a battlemented castle wall but in truth the outer defences of a monastery which here dominates the vine-covered slopes of the hill on which it stands. The castle wall was in fact built in the fifteenth century by Baccio Pontelli and Giuliano da

The romanesque belfry and monastery church of Grottaferrata, seen from the arcaded cloister.

Sangallo on the orders of the future Pope Julius II. Its purpose was to defend an abbey founded in 1104. Great gates protect the narrow arched entrance leading to the interior courtyard, where you can peer through slits in the wall over the surrounding countryside.

Nine hundred years after the founding of this abbey, the monks set up a statue to their patron saint, sculpted by Raffaele Zaccagnini, in the middle of their courtyard. Here, Nilo carries not a crozier but a staff, with a couple of snakes twining round the shaft. I asked one of the monks of Grottaferrata why he was portrayed like this and he replied: 'The saint would plunge his staff in holy water and then bless people with it. The serpents represent devils, who were killed by this holy water.' Was the monk correct, or did he just make up this explanation? I hope he spoke the truth. Certainly these monks know a lot about the symbolism of water. On 6 January, the feast of the Epiphany, they ritually bless the water of their courtyard fountain, in symbolic memory of the baptism of Jesus in the River Jordan.

St Nilo brought into Latin Christendom the Byzantine elements that live on in this monastery. The son of Greek parents who had moved to Calabria, he spent his early life living dissolutely, though for the most part with the unmarried mother of his child. The death of both of them when Nilo was but thirty years old prompted a change of heart. He joined a group of monks dedicated to following the Byzantine rule of St Basil, quitting their company from time to time to live as a hermit. So great became his fame as a spiritual counsellor that many flocked to his monastic home for help and comfort. After he and his fellow Christians had fled from Calabria in the south of Italy to escape the invasion of the Saracens, Nilo still lived as a renowned monk, founding a monastery at Serpero, begging the Emperor Otto not to behave too harshly to a fellow Calabrian and friend who had set himself up as the anti-Pope John XVI.

In 1004 Count Gregory of Tuscolo granted Nilo the land on Monte Cavo on which stands the monastery of Grottaferrata. Alas Nilo never witnessed its foundation, for he died at Frascati on his way here. Today his monastery, though loyal to the papacy, still keeps alive the spirit of Byzantine monasticism and the Byzantine liturgy. Although the simple, six-storeyed campanile is authentically Latin, you can see the Greek influence in the architecture of the place. In 1754 the present church of Santa Maria was rebuilt in the Italian baroque style by Cardinal Bernardi Gaetano Guadagni, yet it preserves its multi-coloured romanesque pavement, its eleventh-century Byzantine mosaics of Jesus, his mother and St Nilo over the doorway of the monastery church, and other eleventh-century mosaics covering the narthex. These blend harmoniously with the superb romanesque heads and animals carved in marble, and with the eleventh-century wooden romanesque doors.

The interior is that of a Greek orthodox church. Its holy of holies is shielded from the body of the building by a baroque iconostasis of 1665, though the chief icon in the sanctuary, that of the thirteenth-century Blessed Virgin, is surrounded by baroque angels and cherubs of a very Roman kind. In the right aisle is an ancient chapel whose windows are closed by iron gratings, or *ferrata*. They derive from a subterranean Roman chamber or grotto, hence the name Grottaferrata. The triumphal arch has not lost its thirteenth-century mosaic depicting the day of Pentecost. The marble font dates from the ninth century. Its carvings depict a man who strips himself of his clothing as if he were casting off his sins, before plunging into the waters and re-appearing as a fish – which in the early church was a symbol of Jesus himself.

To see the most exciting paintings in the church, visitors must find the side chapel dedicated to Saints Nilo and Bartholomew, where frescoes painted in 1610 by Domenico Zampieri (nicknamed Domenichino) recount the life of St Nilo. You can see the artist's self-portrait in the fresco depicting Nilo's meeting with the Emperor Otto III. Domenichino, dressed in greeny-blue shorts and a pink shift, is holding the emperor's white charger. In this holy picture the artist was also moved to include a portrait of his girl friend. She came from Frascati, and Domenichino has painted her face on the boy who is standing apprehensively in front of the horse. The pretty creature wears a blue cap with a white feather.

Here live twenty-five monks, who every Sunday chant a Byzantine-Greek liturgy. Wearing sumptuous vestments, singing ancient chants, they administer the Holy Sacrament in both bread and wine, following the instructions of Jesus himself which the Catholic church has for the most part unaccountably ignored. Small wonder that in 1963 Pope Paul VI came here to make his appeal to the churches of the East to re-unite with the Catholics of western Christendom – an appeal as yet unanswered. Eastern Christians, and others who long for the re-union of Christendom, also come as pilgrims to this spot. Ring the bell and you are admitted to the monastery museum, which opens out onto exquisite cloisters in which grow roses and a couple of palm trees. The museum boasts sarcophagi, Roman remains, antique heads, stained glass and a lovely painted renaissance ceiling. In the library, as you might expect, the monks cherish priceless Greek texts.

Fleeing with his monks from the Saracen invaders, Nilo had taken refuge in a monastery founded by one of the most infuential of all the saints of Christendom. The arch-abbey of Montecassino is recognized as the very cradle of western monasticism. Here in the early sixth century St Benedict of Norcia built a church on the site of a Roman temple. Benedict had been born into a noble family in 480, had studied in Rome and then decided to live as a hermit in a grotto near Subiaco, clad only in a sheepskin cloak. A friend brought him scraps of food, which were let down in a basket to the foot of the cave so that Benedict could be fed while avoiding all human distraction.

In spite of his desire for solitude (and the fact that some shepherds, seeing his bizarre dress and unkempt ways, took him for a wild beast), so many disciples pressed upon St Benedict that eventually he moved with them to the fortified hill of Montecassino, where groves and woods had long been associated with pagan cults. Another reason for leaving Subiaco was that one of his enemies continually introduced into his company a lewd woman, with the aim of seducing the holy man. Overthrowing the pagan temple at Montecassino, Benedict built in its place two chapels, one dedicated to St Michael, the other to St John the Divine. Gradually cells grew around them, filled with the saint's disciples, the core of the future order of Benedictines. Benedict wrote for them a rule of life which still constitutes the basic pattern of the daily ritual of every western monk. He

The Tuscan countryside near the abbey Monte Oliveto Maggiore, south of Siena.

Montecassino, a Benedictine abbey that was destroyed in World War II and has risen again.

taught, as Pope Gregory the Great wrote, 'the way he lived'. His twin sister Scholastica came here with him, insisting on a similar rule for her women followers. Because Montecassino was near enough to Rome, some of the most distinguished men and women of the age became followers of Benedict and his sister.

St Benedict displayed a mercilessly Christian charity, once giving away the entire stores of the monastery to the poor of Campania. He even rebuked Totila the Goth, who was intent on ravaging central Italy. Benedict also foresaw that his monastery would itself be razed. In 577, thirty years after his death, the Lombards destroyed the first monastery of Montecassino. It was restored, the tomb of Benedict was rediscovered and soon pilgrims flocked to venerate his relics. As the centuries progressed, monks of Montecassino achieved the highest offices in the Christian church, the abbey became one of the richest in western Christendom – in manuscripts and learning as well as in conventional wealth — and its abbots were eventually given the honorary title of bishops.

Yet Benedict's vision of the destruction of his foundation came repeatedly to pass. In 1349 an earthquake destroyed Montecassino. Rebuilt, it was decorated by the foremost artists of each successive era. His monastery was looted by revolutionaries in 1799. In the nineteenth century, when many Italian religious houses were suppressed, Montecassino was declared a national monument, to be cared for by its own monks. Then, on 15 February 1944, the commanders of the Allied armies that were driving the Germans from Italy erroneously concluded that the monastery was sheltering enemy soldiers. Bombs destroyed Montecassino. Germans took over the ruins, to be driven out by Polish soldiers three months later.

Today Montecassino has been restored and was reconsecrated by Pope Paul VI in 1964, when he declared that St Benedict of Norcia was henceforth the patron saint of the whole of Europe. Its library of some 80,000 volumes was saved. Beneath it is a war memorial commemorating the 8336 British and commonwealth soldiers who died in World War II. Some of them rest in the nearby cemetery. Here too are German and Polish war cemeteries. Zig-zagging up the hill after the reconstruction of Montecassino, the travel writer Edward Hutton wondered whether he could possibly bear the sight of a reproduction of the monastery he had known for half a century. He found 'a reproduction as near as might be of the abbey that was destroyed in 1944'. The basilica was an exact copy of its predecessor.

Strangely enough, Edward Hutton lamented the fact. In his view it would have been better to have reproduced St Peter's, Rome, at Montecassino. I disagree. To walk up the wooded hillside from the Polish cemetery, where over a thousand soldiers sleep, to the irregular rectangle which constitutes the classical and baroque abbey buildings is to me extraordinarily moving. The stuccoed and marbled church had risen from ashes. St Benedict and St Scholastica once again lie under its high altar. In spite of the destruction of World War II, vestiges of wall dating back to the sixth century BC can still be seen. A loggia such as Bramante might have built overlooks the beautiful Liri plain.

The reconstruction not only followed the design of the sixteenth- and seventeenth-century abbey; the restorers also utilized every fragment of the original stones that they could recover. In consequence, renaissance decoration overseen by Antonio da Sangallo the Younger in 1510 still enriches the renovated cloisters. An early eighteenth-century statue of St Benedict escaped destruction and once again graces his monastery. The façade of the church has been resurrected again in its former baroque glory. In the Capella delle Reliquie three fourteenth-century carvings of the crucified Christ, St Peter and St Paul remind us that the cult of relics is eternal, for alleged fragments of the two saints are also on display here. As for the sixteenth-century crypt, it survived the bombardments intact — though no one can efface the unlovely effect of a so-called restoration of 1913. Finally, where priceless works of religious art had been irretrievably destroyed, twentieth-century artists of the calibre of Pietro Annigoni were commissioned to replace them.

The Benedictine order, like virtually every monastic foundation, occasionally lost its spiritual way, but again and again new ascetic figures arose to bring their fellow-monks back from laxity. One such was St Guglielmo of Montevergine, who was born at Vercilli in Piedmont towards the end of the eleventh century. Orphaned as a child, his foster-parents so inspired him with tales of pilgrimages that at the age of fourteen the lad set off for the great shrine of St James at Santiago de Compostela in Spain. His journey, like that of all contemporary pilgrims to Santiago, involved lodging in monastic hospices, which fired the young man to take up a life of meditation himself — if possible in solitude. Eventually his wanderings brought him to the Campania and to the craggy hills known as the Basilicata. Over the centuries natural erosion, aided by deforestation, have nibbled away at their thick layer of calcareous clay. Frequent landslides have contributed to a hillscape of fissures and craggy white slopes.

Such a terrain seemed to Guglielmo ideal for the life of a hermit. He chose to settle on Montevergine, one of the peaks of Monte Partenio. Long a holy spot, it still carried the ruins of a temple of Cybele where no less a sage than Virgil had come to study the Sybilline Books (the writings of pagan prophetesses which Romans consulted whenever they felt threatened by some new emergency). Guglielmo built himself a cell, but as with many a holy saint and would-be solitary, soon disciples gathered around him. Using stone from the pagan temple, he and his brethren built a sanctuary dedicated to the Virgin Mary, and the Bishop of Avellino consecrated it on Whit Sunday 1124. The monks accepted Guglielmo's example and decided to live by the Rule of St Benedict.

Over the centuries the sanctuary grew rich and famous, enlisting the support of popes and princes. In 1310 Catherine II Valois, married to a prince of the Neapolitan royal family, inherited an icon which had been brought to the west by the Byzantine Emperor Baldwin II, who had been forced to flee from Constantinople when the Greeks took the city in the thirteenth century. Catherine gave the icon to the sanctuary at Montevergine, where nearly thirty years later she was buried. Like the Madonna of Loreto, the icon was attributed to the artist Evangelist, St Luke himself. Scholars, alas, describe it as a thirteenth-century copy of an earlier piece. Even so, the Neapolitans have dubbed the image 'Mamma Schiavona'.

Montevergine was suppressed in the mid nineteenth century but rose again under the inspiration of Pope Leo XIII, pontiff from 1878 to 1903. As it has been for centuries, it is still a place of pilgrimage, above all at Whitsuntide in honour of its original consecration and on 8 September (the feast of the nativity of the Virgin). The 18-kilometre journey from Avellino is along a spectacular road which snakes its way up the 1270-metre mountain on which Montevergine is built, offering stunning views of the surrounding countryside. Today's buildings are not those of Guglielmo's time: an earthquake in the early seventeenth century meant they had to be rebuilt. The gothic entrance to the basilica, rightly sculpted with the arms of the Angevin queen who so enriched the monastery, takes you inside the seventeenth-century 'old church', or *chiesa vecchia*, so called because by the mid twentieth century this pretty baroque building was far too small to accommodate the pilgrims to the shrine. Under Abbot Dom Anselmus Transfiglia a new church was begun, completed between 1952 and

1961. This is the building that now houses the icon of 'Mamma Schiavona'. Linger, however, in the old church, with its Byzantine-romanesque baldacchino dating from the thirteenth century. Covered in mosaics, it was the gift of Charles Martel, the eighth-century ruler of the Franks who preserved much of Europe from the Saracens. The abbot's throne dates from the same century. Catherine II Valois lies in an eighteenth-century tomb accompanied by her children Lodovico and Maria. The pillars which stand behind the high altar almost certainly came from the temple of Cybele which Guglielmo cannibalised when he built his first sanctuary.

The monastery cloisters incorporate a little archaeological museum and art gallery which are worth visiting partly for their Roman, Byzantine and romanesque remains, and especially for a late twelfth-century painting of the Madonna and St Guglielmo, which depicts the saint kneeling before Our Lady and her infant son. The monks also

run a metereological observatory. But their chief work remains to continue the ascetic impetus of their founder Guglielmo. For this reason they are one of the few orders still to forbid women to enter their inner quarters, and indeed allow few other visitors to see their eighteenth-century chapter house and refectory. Their other task is to oversee the pilgrimages to the shrine, one of which was experienced by Edward Hutton on the feast of Corpus Christi in 1956. 'I was motored there from Naples by my friend,' he recalled, 'and heard the Mass of the feast with the *Lauda Sion*, beautifully chanted by the monks in the old abbey church; and with a crowd of people I followed the procession along a pathway strewn with flowers and patterned with rose petals and enlivened with fireworks and thunderflashes, as is customary in Italy.'

Although the *piazzale* offers a fine view of the Avellino valley, before leaving Montevergine climb a further 223 metres to the summit of Monte Partenio for a glorious panorama which extends as far as the Gulf of Naples. The road back to Avellino passes the abbot's winter residence, an elegant house built in 1735 by Dom Antonio Vacaro and today the guardian of the monastic archives and some sixteenth-century Flemish tapestries.

If St Guglielmo of Vercelli was acknowledged as a saint within fifty years of his death, St Rita of Cascia had to wait three and a half centuries for canonization. Rita, who was born in 1377 to a peasant couple who lived in Roccaporena, Umbria, married and bore children, yet secretly longed to enter a convent. Since her family responsibilities prevented this, she prayed for the happy deaths of all of them. In the case of her husband, by all accounts a savage, unfaithful drunkard, Rita's prayer was only half-answered. He was murdered. Then her children died, and at last the widow was admitted to the Augustinian convent of Santa Maria Magdalena at Cascia (though only her persistence forced the other nuns to relax the rule that none but virgins should be their companions).

One day, as she prayed before a crucifix, a thorn from the cruel crown encircling the head of Jesus detached itself and flew into her temple. For the last fifteen years of her life the wound suppurated, and Rita was obliged to live apart from the other sisters to spare them the stench. As she wasted away, she sent for a rose from the garden of the peasant home in which she was born. This rose has become her symbol. Rita died in 1447. On the night of her death the bells of the convent rang out, tolled by unseen hands. Now a remarkable transformation took place. The bodily decay which she had experienced in life ended. Her corpse remained intact, and has done to this day as you can see by visiting her glass coffin in her sanctuary at Cascia. Soon after her death, miracles began to occur on behalf of those who had sought her intercession. Since her own earthly life had been fraught with difficulties, she became known as 'the saint of the impossible, the interceder for the desperate cause'.

A decade after her death Rita was locally so famous that the nuns of Cascia decided to transfer her dead body to a sarcophagus inside their convent church. Yet only in 1626 was she beatified and only in 1900 did Pope Leo XIII declare her a saint. In consequence travellers to the hilltown of Cascia encounter a delicious surprise. The basilica of St Rita is a half-Byzantine, but essentially art-deco church. Finished in 1947

Roccaporena, the birthplace in 1377 of St Rita of Cascia.

189

and approached by colonnades, this sanctuary (along with its monastery, school, orphanage and hospital) rises clean, smooth and white amongst the crumbling medieval stones of the rest of the upper town. Over the doorway a Latin inscription reads:

Hail Rita, prophetess of love and sorrowful wife,
From the Saviour's thorns you were born as a beautiful rose!

I find the façade by Giuseppe Martinenghi impressive. No doubt each visitor will have a personal viewpoint on the artistic merit of the mid twentieth-century frescoes inside, their colours almost the garish tones of a child. I prefer the high altar, and especially its intricate thorny decoration. Pilgrims hasten to the chapel of the saint herself, where Rita's corpse is displayed under glass in a silver reliquary created in 1930. Four angels in golden robes guarding the saint represent the four cardinal virtues. In the lower choir she is depicted kneeling before the crucifix, the whip with which she flagellated herself temporarily set aside while a thorn shoots into her forehead. In the crypt, the altar frontal of the chapel of St Augustine depicts another triumph. Rita was urged by a sadistic mother superior to water a dead tree in the monastery garden. She humbly did so, and the tree burst into life.

Splendid architecture alone remains a sufficient reason for visiting these holy places. No-one should leave St Rita's Cascia without exploring the rest of this hilltown, which derives from the Roman city of Cursula and in the Middle Ages thrived as an independent republic. Cascia has preserved the late fourteenth-century church of Sant'Agostino and, in Piazza Garibaldi, the church of San Francesco. Built in 1442, the latter has a fine portal and, unlike Sant'Agostino, a rose window that the builders bothered to complete. Earlier than both of these is the church of Santa Maria, built in 1300 in good time for the baptism of St Rita. She would not of course have seen the couple of renaissance doorways that now embellish its west façade, nor the elaborate retable inside carved by Camillo and Gaspare Angelucci in the mid sixteenth century. Finally, the fifteenth-century church of Sant'Antonio is blessed with contemporary wall-paintings. In the sacristy one shows a minuscule Rita kneeling before an immense crucified Jesus, who is nonetheless dressed in a robe symbolizing his lordship of the universe.

St Rita has never been forgotten by the faithful, and her shrine today pulsates with their prayers. Other saintly dead sometimes seem to have lost their power of attracting pilgrims. One such lies in the beautiful romanesque cathedral of Ancona. The environs of Ancona, once a superb city overlooking the Adriatic, have been ruined not by tourism but by some of the ugliest suburbs in Italy. Whenever I thread my way through the modern city, Joseph Addison's sage remark continually worms its way into my head. 'Ancona', he wrote, 'looks more beautiful at a distance than when you are in it.' If that statement was true in the early eighteenth century, it is all the more accurate today. If you come to the city from the direction of Loreto, you must persist through a desert of grotesque streets, aiming always for the signs pointing in the direction 'centro'. I do not deny that Ancona possesses a fine sea-front. The coastal road which is known as the Passetto takes you headlong down to a blue sea from one of the sweetest classical

The art deco façade of
St Rita's basilica, Cascia.

monuments I know (built by the architect G. Cirilli in honour of the Italian dead of World War I). But such treats are rare. The only remotely decent way into the city is from Rimini to the north. Whichever way you arrive, eventually you find your way up to the promontory overlooking the sea, bent like an elbow as Pliny the Elder put it, and to the old town centred on the cathedral.

This is an utterly different world from the harsh commercial port below. Ancona cathedral was first built in the fifth century on the site of a pagan temple. Its campanile is massive, the essence of simplicity and purity with a couple of round-arched openings two-thirds of the way up each side, and a wider single opening above them. Sometimes its white stones and those of the cathedral façade gleam golden in the sun.

The present church rose on the site of its early Christian predecessor in the late eleventh and early twelfth centuries. Two pink romanesque lions guard the entrance, their insubstantial backs supporting a massive portico. The porch itself is a sculpted arch, built in the thirteenth century when romanesque was teetering over into gothic. This doorway is supported by no fewer than eighteen slender columns, some of them pink, others marbled, others white, a couple elegantly twisting. The interior of the cathedral is equally dignified, laid out in the form of a Greek cross with a simple groined, twelve-sided cupola, a double apse and, in the crossing, calm, romanesque arches springing from romanesque pillars. The south arm of the cross now houses a fine eighteenth-century altar by Luigi Vanvitelli.

In the crypt lies the body of St Cyriacus, patron saint of the city. I had not expected to find him here, since tradition has it that he died at Rome when the Emperor Diocletian was persecuting Christians in the year 303. History records that Cyriacus and his martyr companions were first buried on the Salarian Way close by the spot where they

This romanesque lion has guarded the entrance to the cathedral of Ancona since the thirteenth century.

died, but a devout lady named Lucina had them exhumed and taken to her farm on the road to Ostia.

One never knows with such sainted bones. The sixth-century Acts of Cyriacus (which are almost certainly entirely without historical foundation) describe this martyr as a three-year-old infant who died with his mother when he scratched the face of the judge before whom she was brought as a Christian. If this were fact, the adult corpse at Ancona could not be his. Other legends insist that Cyriacus died on a pilgrimage to Jerusalem. Alongside these tales are legendary stories identifying this bishop with Judas Quiriacus, the converted Jew who revealed to the Empress Helena the whereabouts of Jesus's cross, before becoming Bishop of Jerusalem and meeting his death in a riot there around the year 133. My own guess is that we are gazing on the body of a Roman Christian brought here from the catacombs in Rome and identified without much hesitation and with still less historical accuracy as the victim of Diocletian. Presumably at some time in the Middle Ages when the thirst for relics was gathering momentum, the Christians of Ancona bought back the body of what they took to be their former bishop from the descendants of Lucina.

Few today venerate this dusty skeleton, and I had not expected to find it dressed in the garb of a modern bishop. A more authentic glimpse back into the fourth century is found in the diocesan museum near the cathedral, where the sarcophagus of Flavius Gorgonius is decorated with some of the earliest carvings of scenes from the New Testament. Yet St Cyriacus's cathedral is the finest building in the whole of Ancona. From the promontory on which it stands, looking down over the great basin of the modern port, it is easy to imagine oneself back in those days when, as a great maritime power, Ancona grew into a city powerful enough to repulse the onslaughts of the Holy Roman Emperor Frederick Barbarossa, the Turks and the Venetian fleet. Consistently loyal to the papacy, Ancona has remained a pious city to this day. Back in the hubbub of its centre is an imposing late eighteenth-century archway built by the architect C. Marchionni in honour of Pope Pius VI. But you have to thread your way through narrow dark streets to find most of the remaining historic monuments. The most venerable is a barrel-vaulted Roman arch set up to honour the Emperor Trajan (c.53–117), who built the mole that protects Ancona's harbour. Once his arch was decorated with bronzes. Today only the holes where they were attached remain.

The most comical monument in Ancona is the fourteenth-century fountain of the Calamo, where thirteen stone heads puff out their cheeks to spurt water from the spigots that protrude from their mouths. The most delicate is the thirteenth-century romanesque façade of the church of Santa Maria della Piazza in Via della Loggia, whose round arched doorway is decorated with crumbling coils of carved ornament, its half-marbled façade enlivened with little medallions of majolica. Among secular buildings of the same era, Palazzo degli Anziani, designed by Margaritone del Arezzo is a reminder of what Ancona must have looked like in its heyday. It stands in the Piazza Stracca, near the church of Gesù which Luigi Vanvitelli built in 1743.

Another impressive secular building constructed a hundred years or so after the Palazzo degli Anziani is the Palazzo del Governo, a powerful symbol of civic pride rendered even more impressive two centuries later by the reconstruction of the brick-and-stone belfry which rises over its monumental classical entrance. Nearby stands the eighteenth-century baroque church of San Domenico, protected by remnants of Ancona's ninth-century fortifications as well as by an early eighteenth-century statue of Pope Clement XII, who raises his hand in blessing.

Sculptors as well as painters and architects flourished in medieval and renaissance Ancona. Giorgio da Sebenico's fifteenth-century decoration of the Loggia del Mercanti (the former stock exchange), with its statues of hope, strength, justice and charity and its vigorous carving of the knight of Ancona riding into battle, is matched by the magical portal he carved for the west door of the church of San Francesco. Both make one regret that so little survives of the work of this artist.

We twentieth-century pilgrims seek our inspiration mostly from the artistic survivals of earlier ages, rarely expecting a spiritual boost as well, even where these remains are ecclesiastical and where the bones of godly men and women are reverently preserved. Medieval pilgrims by contrast sought both solace and succour from the godly inheritance of the past and above all from the relics of the most illustrious saints, such as St Francis and St James the Great. In a more rationalist age, the Revd Sydney Smith marvelled at what he regarded as the crazed faith which prompted believers even to die for 'absurd lies, little bits of cloth, feathers, rusty nails, splinters, and other invaluable relics'; yet we should remember that for a medieval Christian the search for salvation involved these physical fragments of sanctity, offering as they did a visible link between him or herself and the divine.

Equally, as we sweep along the superb motorways of present-day Italy, we can forget how painfully slow a pilgrimage could be. In consequence the pilgrim needed more than one spiritual boost on the way to such great shrines as Cascia or Assisi (see below). As a result, all along the most frequented routes parish churches offered lesser shrines, each with its holy bone, fingernail or other alleged piece of a saint. At the hilltown of Castelluccio in Umbria, north of Norcia (the birthplace of St Benedict and his sister St Scholastica), we might today prefer the sporting activities which take place in the vast natural amphitheatre of the Piano Grande, but the medieval pilgrim would first hasten to the church of San Giorgio to seek the comfort of the relic of the English patron saint housed inside.

Despite the example of holy men and women like Francis of Assisi and Rita of Cascia, superb Italian shrines did not arise solely because of the godly. Undoubtedly one of the greatest fifteenth-century churchmen was Aeneas Silvius Piccolomini, who in 1458 was elected pope and took the name Pius II. Yet, as the fierce arguments behind the scenes of the conclave which elected him indicate, this man, though dynamic and brilliant, was no saint. His most famous work was a salacious love-story, *Euryalus and Lucretia*. For several years he had been an ally of the anti-Pope Felix V, who was willing to make Piccolomini his secretary even though the future pope was still delaying ordination in order to continue enjoying a dissolute way of life.

As pope, Piccolomini devoted much of his energy to combating the Turks, who had captured Constantinople in 1453, and he died at Ancona in 1463 while leading the third

Castelluccio, seen against the snow-covered Sibylline hills.

crusade against them. Of his many works, his supreme gift to posterity is in my view architectural. Piccolomini had been born in the little hilltown of Corsignano, 52 kilometres south of Siena. On becoming pope he determined to transform his modest birthplace into a superbly up-to-date cathedral city, charging the architect Bernardo Gamberelli, who was known as Rossellino, to recreate it. In short, Piccolomini decided to create a shrine not to a saint, but to himself.

In 1462 he renamed his birthplace Pienza. There Rossellino built a cathedral, giving it one of the first renaissance façades in Tuscany (though the interior is gothic). The coat of arms of Pius II adorns its pediment, and the cathedral square is named Piazzo Pio II. Even the well in the middle of the piazza was designed by Rossellino, for this city is remarkable in embodying one overriding architectural vision. Rossellino it was who employed such masters as Giovanni di Paolo and Matteo di Giovanni to decorate the

altarpieces of his cathedral. Lorenzo Vecchietta contributed a strikingly animated *Assumption*, Sano di Pietro a *Madonna and Saints*. Rossellino himself designed the gothic choir-stalls. In the same square he built the glorious Palazzo Piccolomini, modelled in part on the Palazzo Rucelli of his own birthplace, Florence. Naturally the papal bedroom inside contains a portrait of Pius II. Its three-tiered loggia looks down onto a hanging garden and across the Orcia valley to the far blue haze of Monte Amiata.

East of the trapezoid piazza stands the gothic Palazzo Vescovile, which Piccolomini presented to the Spaniard Roderigo Borgia, later to be Pope Alexander VI. Even this gift was a calculated thanks-offering, for Roderigo was a nephew of Pope Callixtus III who had made both him and Piccolomini cardinals in 1456. On the north side of the piazza rises a third superb palace, the three-arched, crenellated Palazzo Comunale which was built in 1463. The pope also persuaded both Cardinal Francesco Gonzaga and Jean Jouffroy, Bishop of Arras, to join his project. The palaces they built stand at the eastern end of the main street of Pienza.

Piccolomini's papal cope is displayed today in the Palazzo Canonici which now serves as the city museum. Here too hang a fastidious *Madonna* by Vecchietta (who also painted a sumptuous *Assumption* for Pienza cathedral in 1462) and a *Madonna of Mercy* painted about fifty years earlier by his fellow Sienese Bartolo di Fredi. Although determined to impose his own flamboyant style on the new city, Rossellino was no architectural vandal, and from old Corsignano he preserved the early gothic church of San Francesco, with its fourteenth- and fifteenth-century frescoes and a *Madonna* by Luca Signorelli. He also kept the church where Piccolomini was baptized, the romanesque Pieve di San Vito dell'Antica Corsignano with its pretty round tower, standing a kilometre outside the city to the south. Pius II was so proud of his magnificent new city that when he learned that Rossellino had greatly overspent his budget, the pope praised his architect instead of rebuking him, adding, 'Had you told me the truth you would never have induced me to spend so much money, so that neither my palace nor my cathedral, the finest in all Italy, would today be standing.'

The validity of the papal office, so Catholic theologians wisely remind us, does not depend upon the sanctity or otherwise of its incumbents. Of all the papal shrines of Italy, the Vatican city itself has been the most enriched by the benefactions of illustrious princes of the church, only some of whom should be dubbed saints. Covering a mere 44 hectares and standing on a hill which the Etruscans colonized and Caligula had used for a circus, this spot is infinitely more than a tourist attraction. The great basilica has long been venerated by the faithful as the last resting-place of the mortal remains of St Peter, whatever historians and archaeologists might say. Curiously enough, in our own century the sceptical have been coming round to the view that the faithful may be right. After years of excavations under St Peter's, Rome, Pope Pius XII in 1949 was asked, 'Has the tomb of St Peter really been found here?' and answered, 'Beyond all doubt, yes.' To a second question, 'Have the relics of St Peter himself been found?' he answered, with admirable precision, 'At the side of the tomb human bones have been discovered, though it is impossible to prove that they belong to the body of the apostle.'

The rich countryside around Pienza, the birthplace of Pius II.

197

Nonetheless, since the second century the belief that St Peter's bones lie here has proved a well-spring of devotion, to which the great church of San Pietro is a magnificent monument. This reason alone is enough to account for the vast crowd which assembles in Bernini's huge, colonnaded, elliptical piazza at midday on Sundays to hear a few words from the reigning pontiff and to receive his blessing. By a treaty of 1920 the Italian government has recognized the Vatican city as a sovereign and independent state inside Rome, the smallest in the world, while the papacy in return has recognized Rome as the capital of Italy.

The basilica of San Pietro in Vaticano is the largest in the world, twice the size of Notre-Dame in Paris. In 1452 Pope Nicholas V commissioned Bernardo Rossellino to build it on a spot already redolent with holiness. In its predecessor on Christmas day 800 Charlemagne had been crowned Holy Roman Emperor by Pope Leo III. Work soon fell into abeyance, to be taken up again by such masters as Donato d'Angelo Bramante, Raphael, Baldassare Peruzzi and Giuliano da Sangallo. Michelangelo not only contributed the basic design of its massive dome but also sculpted its celebrated *Pietà*, as well as designing the uniform still worn by the pope's Swiss guards.

Pope Urban VIII consecrated St Peter's on 18 November 1626, since when it has been the Mecca of the western Catholic world. Inside the church, the kisses of multitudes have polished the toe of the famous thirteenth-century bronze statue of St Peter. Bernini's sinuous baldacchino, imitated by hundreds of his successors, is by no means the only masterpiece he contributed to this cathedral. He created the monument to Urban VIII in the choir and the bronze 'pulpit of St Peter' in the apse. From an earlier age comes Pollaiuolo's 1498 monument to Innocent VIII, and in the eighteenth century Canova contributed a smoothly sumptuous statue of Clement XIII.

The French novelist Stendhal (Henri Beyle) visited Rome in 1827 and wisely observed that, 'If a foreigner enters St Peter's and attempts to see everything he will develop a furious headache, and soon satiety and pain will render him incapable of any pleasure.' Stendhal's advice was, 'Allow yourself only a few moments to indulge in the admiration inspired by a monument so great, so beautiful, so well-kept, in a word the most beautiful church in the most beautiful region in the world.' Perhaps a little more than a few moments is called for, but in a spot so wealthy in great monuments his note of caution is worth repeating. As for the eleven Vatican museums and five Vatican art galleries, their riches are beautifully displayed in some 1400 rooms, and once again Stendhal's caveat needs to be remembered. Between 1498 and 1517 Raphael and his pupils decorated the salon of Pope Julius II. Rightly the most celebrated masterpiece is Michelangelo's decoration of the Sistine Chapel, his figures mostly voluptuously naked (especially the males among them) and all of them today becoming more glorious as restorers reach the conclusion of their stupendous project.

We also owe to the papacy many of the delights of grey-walled Castelgandolfo just outside Rome, built above the volcanic crater that is now the Lake of Albano. It stands on the site of the ancient Roman town of Alba Longa, and legend asserts that the town was founded by Ascanius, the son of Aeneas. In addition, Castelgandolfo claims to be the birthplace of Romulus and Remus, twin sons of Mars and a princess of these parts,

199

and legendary founders of Rome. Today it is better known as the summer residence of the pope, which it has been since 1604. Standing on the belvedere you can understand why his holiness chose this spot. Woods of oak and chestnut surround the lake and climb the slopes of Monte Cavo across the water. At its summit rises the remains of a temple of Jupiter. So ancient are some of the trees adjoining Castelgandolfo that a group of them has been designated a national monument.

Papal patronage has transformed this hilltown without destroying its charm. Perhaps there is just a tiny surfeit of papal plaques plastering the *palazzo* walls, where the tiara and crossed keys ornament the coats of arms of Clement XII, Alexander VII, Paul V and Urban VIII, and an inscription of 1947 describes Pius XII as 'defender of the fatherland'. Still, these popes helped to enhance Castelgandolfo. The seventeenth-century Palazzo dei Papa stands where the Gandolfi family built their twelfth-century castle, thus giving the hilltown its name; but what we admire today is a beautifully ordered building designed five centuries later by Stefano Maderno for Pope Urban VIII. It even hosts an observatory, the Specula Vaticana.

In the early seventeenth century the same Pope Urban VIII commissioned landscape gardeners to surround his palace with lawns and hedges. Lorenzo Bernini, ever assiduous to glamorize papal residences, added not only a monumental staircase to the palace but also contributed the fountain opposite the castle in the Piazza della Libertà, a strangely gentle work from such a flamboyant architect. As for Bernini's church of San Tommaso da Vilanova, its treasures include paintings by Pietro da Cortona and Ambrogio da Borgognone, and its beauty derives from the architect's skill in executing one of his favourite ground plans: a Greek cross. His extreme lightness of touch has created a beautiful building, with an ogival dome rising from Doric pillars. Inevitably, the coat of arms of Alexander VII placards its entrance.

Two scenic routes leave this hilltown. Via dei Laghi takes you upwards to a church which once belonged to a thirteenth-century convent, lay-bys along the road giving opportunities to pause and drink in the view over the lake. The second route is known as the Bivio and curls its way down from Castelgandolfo to the water's edge.

As Robert Browning put it, 'Everyone soon or later comes round by Rome.' But Assisi, and not Rome, is the Italian pilgrimage city which ultimately I return to, in spite of the throngs of tourists and the religious knick-knacks of the obtrusive trinket shops which here must surely offend believer and unbeliever alike. The charm of St Francis (1182–1226) remains irresistible. Born into wealth and embracing poverty, this was a saint who cultivated austerity yet never lost his love of singing. He was half-French, inheriting the blood of Picardy troubadours from his mother. His father's riches allowed the young Francis to flaunt himself as the glittering leader of the gilded youth of Assisi. He fought for Assisi against Perugia and was for a time a prisoner of war. What brought him to reconsider his life was first sickness and then a miracle. In the church of San Damiano the crucifix seemed to speak to him as he prayed, ordering him to repair a ruined chapel which was an offence to God.

Soon Francis was spending his father's wealth on repairing not one ruined church but two and then three. When his enraged father summoned his son to a confrontation in the presence of the Bishop of Assisi, the future saint calmly stripped himself naked and gave all his clothing back to his father. Henceforth he dressed in rags, making a pilgrimage to Rome where he embraced an emaciated leper.

On his return to Assisi, Francis and a few followers set themselves up as hermits. Their cells centred around a little chapel that probably dated from the fourth century. Today a massive, triple-naved basilica stands on this spot, built between 1569 and 1679 to the designs of Gian Galeazzo Alessi. Inside you find the tiny chapel whose name, the Porziuncola, means 'little place'. Francis had found it abandoned and restored it in the early years of his new life. This spot was where he was professed as a monk in 1208. Here his first followers took their vows; and in 1211 the Porziuncola was where the saint invested as a nun St Clare, foundress of the order of poor Clares.

Francis also died here, on 3 October 1226, aged only forty-four. This sanctuary is thus amongst the holiest in Christendom. Virtually unchanged since Francis left this earthly life, its tranquillity is an enormous relief from the basilica that houses it, especially since the megalomaniac architect Cesare Bazzanti added a new façade in 1927, topped by an oversized gilded statue of the Virgin Mary. Far more in keeping with the spirit of St Francis and the unpretentious beauty of the Porziuncola is the polyptych behind the high altar, depicting scenes from the saint's life and painted by a monk of Viterbo little more than a century and and half after Francis's death.

Seek out too the little rose garden attached to the church where there are blossoms with blood-red streaks but no thorns. Francis, the story runs, once was so tormented by the desires of the flesh that he leapt into a thorny rose to control himself. Unwilling to harm the saint in any way, the bush is said to have instantly shed its thorns. Certainly the rose bushes outside the Porziuncola have followed suit.

His body no longer lies here but in the huge double basilica of San Francesco, which towers above the site of the Porziuncola and the medieval gateway of San Pietro, $4\frac{1}{2}$ kilometres away at Assisi itself. San Francesco is called a double basilica because one church has been literally built on top of another. On 25 May 1230 the body of St Francis, canonized two years previously, was reverently borne to the lower church, to be interred in the crypt. As you enter this building through a shaded gothic porch, you see on your left the saint's tattered robe, displayed amongst a few of his other possessions. I have seen a similar one in Florence (in the church of Ognissanti), so Francis must have possessed at least two. The Florentines claim that theirs was being worn by the saint in September 1224 when he received the stigmata of his Lord on the mountain of La Verna; but who is to know? At any rate the basilica at Assisi also possesses his body, housed in a splendid shrine along with the remains of four of his earliest followers (Brother Leo, Brother Masso, Brother Angelo and Brother Rufino). Here today countless pilgrims kneel before his shrine. They have done so for little more than a century and a half, for the medieval authorities were so concerned that grave-robbers would steal the saint's relics that they hid them. Later generations forgot where they were concealed, and the dusty bones were recovered only in 1818.

Alas, few truly pray in this sanctuary. Many in my observation simply chatter and take photographs. I have seen the same impious phenomenon in the chapel of the

OVERLEAF
The basilica and convent of San Francesco, Assisi, set against Monte Subiaso.

sacred corporal at Orvieto. Although notices enjoin strict silence, I watched a French priest guide his faithful flock around the sacred spot with expressive gestures and a garrulous commentary. In consequence, perhaps the real bones of the saint have flown from Assisi, for certainly excavations in 1978 found not the corpse of a man bearing the stigmata but only an unidentifiable skeleton.

No matter: his spirit lives on here, and his life has inspired the great works of art which decorate both the lower and the upper basilica, the two most notable the frescoes by Cimabue and Giotto. On the wall of the right transept of the lower basilica Cimabue painted an enthroned Madonna. She is flanked by four angels. Accompanying them is Francis, looking unusually sad. Giotto's opportunity was created by an architect whose name has been forgotten. This genius built the upper basilica in the early thirteenth century, a masterpiece of Umbrian gothic whose wall spaces might have been created for Giotto's twenty-eight scenes from the life of Francis (though Cimabue and his apprentices also managed to cover some of the walls). Giotto clearly warmed to some episodes in the life of his subject. Francis, it is said, used to preach to the birds as well as to his fellow Christians. Sure enough Giotto has painted these attentive creatures. He has also depicted the saint stripping off his clothing, the Bishop of Assisi averting his gaze with embarrassment as he offers the naked Francis a blue towel. The saint's father, by contrast, seems ready to hit his son across the face.

The white stones of the basilica serenely reflect the Umbrian sun, a magnificent rose window above the main double door flanked as in many an Umbrian romanesque church with the symbols of the four Evangelists. Inside, stained-glass windows of the

LEFT
The *duomo* of Assisi displays its romanesque façade and stern campanile.

RIGHT
The church of Santa Chiara, Assisi, supported by monumental flying buttresses.

thirteenth and fourteenth centuries shed multi-coloured light on the worshippers. Fortunately people do not chatter incessantly in every part of the basilica, and the feeling of peace I derive from visiting this spot does not desert me as I climb up to the bustling centre of Assisi, the irregular Piazza del Comune. Its finest monuments are the battlemented tower of the Palazzo del Capitano del Popolo, built between 1212 and 1305 and, nearby, the remarkably perfect Roman temple of Minerva which now calls itself the church of St Philip Neri. Further on is a church that is unjustly forgotten because of Francis's double basilica. San Rufino is Assisi's cathedral. Its façade boasts not one but three rose windows, the centre one, as at the basilica of San Francesco, guarded by the symbols of the Evangelists. Below them runs an elegant loggietta. To the left of the cathedral rises a thunderingly powerful romanesque campanile.

Nor can we forget St Clare. Pink, violet and white marble from Monte Subiaso, whose mass protects Assisi from the harsh east winds, provided the delicate hues of the thirteenth-century façade of the church of Santa Chiara, with a row of massive arched buttresses on the north side. Clare's remains lie in the crypt. And here too is the crucifix of San Damiano which once talked to St Francis.

Almost everywhere you walk in Assisi his spirit reappears. A stroll down Via Sant'Agnese from Santa Chiara (the street is named after St Clare's sister) leads to the Piazza Vescovado, a medieval balcony which overlooks a green Umbrian valley. The pine-studded *campania* stretches out to maybe seven or eight ridges of hills in the distance. Swallows dart through the air. One can understand how the citizens would feel secure inside the walls of the city, protected by the formidable *rocca* dating from the fourteenth century which looks down on the town and able to see the approach of any enemy miles away. Here stands an eleventh-century church whose rose window is not only inscribed with its date (1163) but also the name of the mason who designed it (Giovanni da Gubbio). Close by is the episcopal palace, where Francis shed his garments. And as if to demonstrate how the charity of this saint has lived on in the people of Assisi, in the same square rises the tower of a nunnery dedicated to San Giuseppe whose order hid persecuted Jews during the fascist tyranny in World War II.

Of such figures from the past as Francis and Clare the historian G. M. Trevelyan in his unbelieving days wrote that these were men and women who lived and breathed like ourselves and now are gone, like ghosts at cockcrow. It could be of course that they are alive in heaven. I am certain that their shadows linger on in Assisi. And the first poem ever written in the Italian tongue, troubadour St Francis's canticle of the creatures, seems also to rejoice in the beauty of the surrounding countryside which he must often have gazed on from the walls of his hilltown:

> *Laudato si mi signore per sora nostra matre terra,*
>    *la quale ne sustenta et governa,*
>       *et produce diversi fructi con colorati fiori et herba.*

> Praise to Thee my Lord for our sister Mother Earth,
>    who nourishes and sustains us all,
>       and brings forth diverse fruits with many coloured flowers and herbs.

# INDEX